OSPREY COMBAT AIRCRAFT • 95

VALIANT UNITS
OF THE COLD WAR

SERIES EDITOR: TONY HOLMES

OSPREY COMBAT AIRCRAFT • 95

VALIANT UNITS OF THE COLD WAR

ANDREW BROOKES

OSPREY
PUBLISHING

Front Cover
The first real British hydrogen bomb was dropped from Valiant XD825 on an offshore point southeast of Christmas Island, in the Pacific Ocean, on 8 November 1958. Known as *Grapple 'X'*, it was released from 45,000 ft by Sqn Ldr Barney Millett's crew, with bomb-aimer Frank Corduroy dropping visually from the nose prone position using a T4 bombsight. The rest of the cockpit was already blacked out by metal shutters, and after Corduroy pressed the bomb release and felt the weapon go, he put the last screen up. Barney Millett pulled XD825 round into the standard escape manoeuvre, consisting of a 60-degree banked 1.7 G turn to port through 130 degrees, while slightly descending to increase speed. The two-stage thermonuclear bomb exploded with a force of 1.8 megatons (MT) at around 8000 ft. The slant range between XD825 and the air burst was just under nine nautical miles. Derek Tuthill, Nav Plotter on the Millett crew, recalled;

'Soon after takeoff we were advised that the drop had been delayed because a ship had entered the target area. We carried out practice runs until the vessel was clear. We knew that we wouldn't see any flash with the screens up. We just waited for the shockwave, which came some two-and-a-half minutes after weapon release. It was definitely noticeable, but a non-event compared with rolling a Canberra! We all had great faith in Frank Corduroy who'd been a B-29 Washington bomb-aimer on No 35 Sqn. My main thought was "Thank God it had all gone to plan".'

Grapple 'X' was spectacularly successful, exceeding the predicted yield of 1 MT by almost 80 per cent. As the Millett crew flew XD825 back over an empty Pacific Ocean to land on Christmas Island, Britain had become a true thermonuclear power (*Cover artwork by Gareth Hector*)

Title page Spread
Valiant B 1 XD824 looks sleek without drop tanks – the Vickers bomber was rarely seen in flight without the latter stores. This aircraft participated in the *Grapple* trials whilst assigned to No 49 Sqn

For Katharine and Christina
First published in Great Britain in 2012 by Osprey Publishing
Midland House, West Way, Botley, Oxford, OX2 0PH
44-02 23rd Street, Suite 219, Long Island City, NY, 11101, USA

E-mail; info@ospreypublishing.com

Osprey Publishing is part of the Osprey Group

A CIP catalogue record for this book is available from the British Library

ISBN: 978 1 84908 753 7
e-book PDF ISBN: 978 1 84908 754 4
e-pub ISBN: 978 1 78096 118 7

Edited by Tony Holmes
Page design by Tony Truscott
Cover Artwork by Gareth Hector
Aircraft Profiles by Chris Davey
Index by Michael Forder
Originated by PDQ Digital Media Solutions, Suffolk, UK
Printed in China through Bookbuilders

12 13 14 15 16 10 9 8 7 6 5 4 3 2 1

Osprey Publishing is supporting the Woodland Trust, the UK's leading woodland conservation charity, by funding the dedication of trees.

www.ospreypublishing.com

Acknowledgements
This book could not have been written without the help of all the Valiant 'old and bold' who gave so unstintingly of their time and patience. I cannot mention them all by name, but my particular thanks must go to John Matthews, Pete Sharp and Robin 'Nobby' Unwin, who kept me firmly on track.

CONTENTS

BIRTH OF A BOMBER

The draft Operational Requirement (OR) that led to the creation of the RAF V-bombers was first circulated on 7 November 1946. In it, the Air Staff required 'a medium-range bomber landplane capable of carrying one 10,000-lb bomb [the weight of the first British atom bomb, called Blue Danube] to a target 1500 nautical miles from a base which may be anywhere in the world'.

The new bomber differed from its wartime predecessors in that it was to be powered by jet engines, it was to carry no protective gun turrets and the crew of five was to be housed in a single pressure cabin designed for high-altitude flight. 'We stretched the elastic a bit', recalled Sir Geoffrey Tuttle, Director of Operational Requirements in 1948-49, 'so that we were stretching industry, Farnborough and everybody else in time and in technique'.

This OR grew into Specification B 35/46, which dictated that the cruising speed was to be 575 mph (Mach 0.875 in the stratosphere), and the aircraft was to be capable of reaching 50,000 ft within two-and-a-half hours of takeoff. It was hoped that the bomber would exceed 50,000 ft by as great a margin as possible as weight reduced. Spec B 35/46 preferred that the aircraft had no fewer than four and not more than six engines, and stipulated that it must be operable from existing bomber airfields. 'Catapult or trolley launching is not acceptable, nor is arrestor gear for landing'.

B 35/46 called for a high degree of manoeuvrability at height and speed, provision for adequate warning and radio countermeasures equipment and space for installing tail armament should the arguments against carrying orthodox defensive weaponry prove to be invalid. The aircraft was to have an all-weather capability centred upon the H2S radar – that wartime product of British electronic genius which gave crews such a good blind-bombing capability that they could pick out individual buildings at night from more than 20,000 ft.

The whole aircraft was to be designed for large-scale production in wartime, with an economic output of at least 500 aircraft at a rate of no fewer than ten per month. The strategic concept in 1947 therefore was still one of the peacetime services acting as an 'expanding nucleus' in time of war.

Blue Danube, the first British operational atomic bomb, is seen here on display outside the Bomber Command Armament School at Wittering. The magnitude of the weapon, which had to fit in the Valiant bomb-bay, can be judged by the size of the warrant officer standing far right.

On 9 January 1947 six firms were invited to tender for the B 35/46 bomber that was to be operational in ten years time. The most uncomplicated shapes were the English Electric submission, looking very much like a scaled-up Canberra, and the Vickers proposal incorporating the longest fuselage of all supported by a high aspect ratio wing of about 26 degrees sweep. These, it was quickly decided, were not advanced enough for the needs of 1957, and they were discarded. But the other four were futuristic enough for anyone. Pronounced sweepback, deltas, crescents, flying wings – the full panoply of advanced aeronautics – were all there, and they were too much for an Air Ministry that had only just accepted the Avro Lincoln into operational service. Consequently, the Director of Royal Aircraft Establishment (RAE) Farnborough asked the head of his Aerodynamic Flight Section, 35-year-old Welshman Morien Morgan, to chair an Advanced Bomber Project Group with a brief to choose between the advanced bomber shapes as a matter of urgency.

When the RAE set up an Advanced Fighter Project Group in November 1948 to decide on the fighter of the future, it recommended only one choice – the English Electric Lightning. Life was not so straightforward for the Advanced Bomber Group, and it concluded that 'because of the present uncertainty of basic information, we cannot put all our eggs into one basket. Several designs must be chosen in order to spread the risk'. These were the crescent-wing Handley Page HP 80 and the tailless delta Avro 698. The HP 80 promised to fly higher – 52,500 ft, compared with approximately 48,500 ft for the Avro 698 – but the delta design was much more manoeuvrable at height.

The two designs complemented one another, but the Project Group recommended them both in case one turned out to possess some ghastly fault at height that would render it unworkable. To spread the risk still further the Project Group also suggested an intermediate simpler-tailed aircraft with an aspect ratio of four and less sweepback. 'Such an aircraft would in our view be the most satisfactory compromise between the two extremes, and would be particularly valuable if sweepback were not as effective as was hoped in postponing critical Mach number'.

Spec B 35/46 had included provision for such an interim insurance aircraft to give Bomber Command a low-cost, jet-propelled replacement to replace the Lincoln. Known as B 14/46, this specification for a 'simple' interim jet bomber with lower ceiling and speed was issued to Short Brothers on 11 August 1947. Range, radius of action and bomb load were to be the same as B 35/46, but Short's bomber, known as the SA 4, was designed without wing sweep around a top speed of Mach 0.81. Following the appearance at Farnborough in 1951, the SA 4 was christened Sperrin after the lofty mountain range dividing the counties of Londonderry and Tyrone.

But the Sperrin was effectively only a World War 2 bomber with jet engines. Even if Mach 0.81 had been attainable with the prototype – which it was not because aileron flutter above 42,000 ft limited the top speed to Mach 0.78 – this was not really good enough for the nuclear age. The more the RAF looked at the Sperrin, the more it became clear that it needed something that could fly higher and faster. This in turn meant something more sophisticated than the Short bomber, which had yesterday's aerodynamics written all over it.

That there was something else immediately available to bridge the gap between the Lincoln and the two advanced bomber extremes was due entirely to the drive and salesmanship of one man, George R Edwards. Born on 9 July 1908, George Edwards was educated at London University. After a period in industrial engineering, he decided to 'have a go' at aeroplanes at the end of 1934. Joining Vickers-Armstrong at Weybridge as an aircraft stressman, Edwards became Experimental Works Manager in 1940, and made such an impression that he was appointed Chief Designer in the autumn of 1945 at the tender age of 37.

The war ended for Vickers with its workshops filled with Warwick and Wellington bombers. The company's first post-war airliner was the Viking, from which came the Valetta and Varsity, but times were tough for the firm by 1947. Despite orders from airlines overseas, British European Airways had apparently killed Vickers' turboprop-powered Viscount airline project at birth by ordering a fleet of 23 Airspeed Ambassadors. There was only a limited future for the Viking family, and Vickers' total production was down by a half.

The company's original submission for the advanced bomber had been turned down on the grounds of lack of sophistication, but George Edwards kept his foot in the Whitehall door, from where he argued that this apparent disadvantage was in fact his aircraft's greatest asset. In his view the complicated and novel Handley Page and Avro offerings stood as much chance of not working as of meeting the specification, whereas the Vickers design, with its limited sweepback, was perfectly capable of achieving the requirements of B 14/46. Moreover, it was much simpler and easier to build, being based on today's technology rather than on tomorrow's. George Edwards' theme was that the advanced bombers were the creation of theorists going too far ahead too quickly, and that the UK could get something virtually as good, with no risk, much quicker because he could guarantee to get the Vickers bomber into service long before the advanced types.

This argument appealed to the powers that be, and the Advanced Bomber Project Group was told to look into it. It, in turn, felt that it was up to the RAF to judge the urgency of the situation, and that if the air force wanted a long-range high-performance jet bomber quickly then the Vickers submission, known as the Type 660, with its smaller sweep and fewer development problems, was a viable proposition. 'We could see nothing to be said for the Sperrin', recalled Morien Morgan. 'It seemed an awful botch, a very inferior article, and we didn't like that at all'. The Sperrin was doomed from February 1948 when Morgan's group published its report. Two Sperrin prototypes saw out their days as flying test-beds, with one dropping concrete dummies of the Blue Danube 10,000-lb atom bomb. The whole Sperrin programme cost £3.5 million, but it answered some of the questions that perplexed designers in 1946, even if, in the process, it damned itself as inadequate. From then on the 'interim' aircraft was to be the Vickers 660.

Vickers was cleared to proceed on 16 April 1948. A new specification, B 9/48, was issued on 19 July 1948 that sought a bomber of conventional design with a range of not less than 3350 nautical miles at a height of 40,000 ft and a speed of 653 mph. B 9/48 took Edwards at his word and committed Vickers to producing a first flying prototype no later than

1951 and, even more demanding, an airborne production machine before the end of 1953. In return the RAF got Vickers' original B 35/46 submission that had been modified to include an expanded root chord between the fuselage and main part of the wing, as this was now seen as necessary to make the initial concept work.

The Type 660, which became the Vickers Valiant, was the first aircraft George Edwards oversaw from beginning to end. Of all the aircraft with which he was to be involved, the Valiant was the one he was most proud and fond of. 'GRE', as he was known throughout the industry, came up with the design after sifting through all the latest technology that the world had to offer, and he concluded that the single-curvature wing was the best shape for the good, reliable and easy-to-build bomber he had in mind.

'The Valiant was George Edwards' aircraft alright', said Morien Morgan, 'but without the host of eager beavers around him, who were all men of substance in their own right, he would have been stuck'. There was Ernie Marshall in charge of the Project Office who, with George Edwards, put down on paper the shape that was to become the Valiant. When this left the Project Office for the Drawing Office, George Edwards knew he had three excellent assistant chief designers to take it over for him. These were Basil Stephenson, in charge of structures, Henry Gardner, looking after stress, and aerodynamicist Elfyn Richards, who devised the Valiant's 'compound sweep' configuration with a 37-degree angle of sweepback in the inner third of the wing, reducing to an angle of about 21 degrees at the tips. It was men such as these who, through their own abilities and hard toil, made the Valiant work.

The design took shape at Vickers' wartime site of Fox Warren, rather than in the company's main Weybridge, Surrey, factory. Here, amid fir trees in a 'secure establishment', two Type 660 prototypes took shape in 1950 under the careful eye of A E 'Charlie' Houghton. These were built in the Fox Warren experimental shop firstly for security reasons, secondly because Weybridge was full of Viscounts, Valettas and Vikings and thirdly because it was halfway to Wisley airfield, from where they were to be test-flown.

There was a constant shuttle of lorries out to Fox Warren, where the wings, fuselage, fin and tailplane for the prototypes were made and assembled. Today, aircraft firms use welded jigs, but in the days of austerity and raw material shortages of 1950, the team at Fox Warren had to use jigs made out of ordinary builders' scaffolding. From here the major sections were transported down the Portsmouth Road to Wisley, often in the quiet of the early morning hours, to be assembled ready for the first prototype flight on 18 May 1951.

Capt Joseph 'Mutt' Summers had been Vickers' Chief Test Pilot since 1929, and he was determined to fly the prototype Valiant before he retired. 18 May 1951 proved to be a gusty day, but this did not prevent Summers and G R 'Jock' Bryce taking the Type 660 prototype, WB210, on a maiden flight that lasted all of five minutes. As a normal precautionary measure the undercarriage was locked down and the flaps, set at 20 degrees for takeoff, were not selected up during the trip. Vickers had beaten the first Sperrin into the air by three months.

On 19 February 1951 V E Bass from the Ministry of Supply had written that 'an official designation is required for the B 9/48 aircraft'.

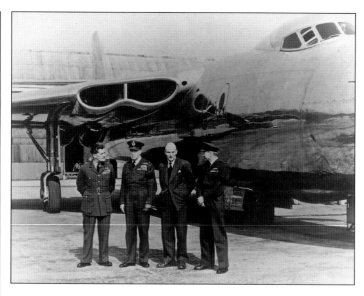

The second Valiant prototype, WB215, after roll out at Weybridge in April 1952. Standing in front of the aircraft are, from left to right, AVM Geoffrey Tuttle (Assistant Chief of Air Staff (Operational Requirements)), Air Chief Marshal Sir Hugh Lloyd (C-in-C Bomber Command), George Edwards (Chief Designer) and AVM George Harvey (Senior Air Staff Officer, Bomber Command). They are wearing black armbands in mourning for King George VI

Second prototype WB215 with long-range drop tanks during preparations for the New Zealand Air Race in 1953. Eventually WB215 was pulled out of the event because it was unable to complete enough flight test hours for the Air Ministry to authorise its participation

Up to now it had been policy to name RAF bombers after 'an inland town of the British Commonwealth or associated with British history'. However, scribbled on Mr Bass's letter were the names Vulcan, Veesign, Veidae, Vancouver, Veejayday and Vimy (which was ringed). This suited the firm, as apart from the Barnes Wallis era, when its bomber names began with 'W', most of Vickers' aircraft began with 'V' for alliterative effect.

On 6 March Vickers replied that it would like to use the name Vimy, but no more was heard until 30 July, when the company was informed, 'Will you please note that the official nomenclature for the production B 9/48 is Valiant B Mk 1', resurrecting the name used for a single-engined two-seater general purpose military biplane of 1927. In 1952, when names for the B 35/46 bombers were being discussed in the Air Council, the Chief of Air Staff (CAS), Marshal of the RAF Sir John Slessor, said that his inclination was 'to establish, so to speak, a V class of medium jet bombers'.

At the Farnborough airshow of 1951, Jock Bryce, who took over as Vickers' Chief Test Pilot when 'Mutt' Summers retired, unveiled the Valiant to the world. The Short Sperrin that preceded it in the display, flown by Tom Brooke-Smith, thundered down the runway and did a slow circuit of the airfield with the flaps extended, but there was nothing exciting about it. One magazine correspondent compared it to a Whitley because it flew nose-down in level flight, but no one thought of comparing the Valiant with any of the last generation of aircraft when it took off next. To the audience it looked and climbed like a fighter, and in Jock Bryce's hands the Valiant exuded grace and power, even though he was obviously holding back the as yet relatively untested aircraft. When airshow commentator Oliver Stewart pointed out that a Valiant with an atom bomb packed a bigger punch than a battleship, he was echoing the pride of many in the symbol of a new era.

Flight testing of WB210 continued until 12 January 1952, when the prototype was sent to carry out engine relight tests over the Hampshire coast in connection with the V 1000 projected military transport derivative of the Valiant. One Avon engine suffered a wet start and caused a fire in a bay where no detection system had been thought necessary, and by the time it was discovered the crew

thought the wing was about to come off. Everyone escaped except the co-pilot, Sqn Ldr B H D Foster (Bomber Command's liaison officer at Vickers), who ejected while the aircraft was in a descending turn. He was killed when he struck the fin because his ejection seat had the wrong explosive charges fitted. Modifications to the atmospheric balance in the fuel system that caused the wet start cured this fault.

Back on 9 February 1951, the British government had placed an initial order for 25 Valiants – five pre-production Type 674s and 20

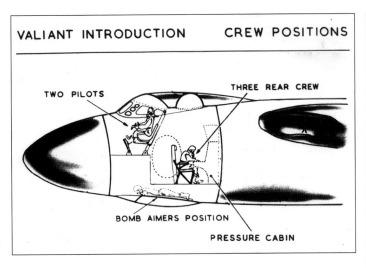

Type 706 production model B Mk 1s. The Valiant had a shoulder wing with compound leading edge sweepback, although the wingtips and trailing edge were both straight. The four engines were housed in the wing, and as the exhaust jet pipes protruded above the trailing edges, the tailplane was mounted halfway up the fin so as to be clear of the jet efflux. Internal fuel tankage in the wings and fuselage was supplemented by large underwing tanks. The Type 674 had four 9500-lb thrust Avon RA 14 engines, while the Type 706 aircraft was cleared to a higher maximum weight of 175,000 lbs thanks to its 10,000-lb thrust Avon RA 28 204 or 205 engines that exhausted through lengthened jet pipes.

Virtually all the airframe was made in the Weybridge workshops, with the exception of the pressure cabin, landing flaps and ailerons, which were subcontracted out to firms such as Fokker. Moreover, Vickers did most of the system installation – not even the RAE was as far ahead in the technology of high-altitude flight as Vickers. All this, plus having to introduce a fairly extensive programme of pre-stressed concrete jigging to compensate for the national shortage of steel brought about by the Korean War, explains how the Valiant was designed, manufactured and put into service so quickly. The flight of the first pre-production Type 674 from Brooklands on 22 December 1953 meant that 'GRE' had fulfilled all his promises with nine days to spare.

How much was the Valiant a jump into the future? As far as George Edwards himself was concerned, it was 'far and away the hardest aeroplane that I ever did'. Much of it was very new – better steels, better aluminium alloys, better paints, better electrics, better everything – but although the Valiant stretched Vickers to its

This Vickers drawing shows the crew positions in the Valiant B 1

The Valiant production line at Weybridge in early 1955

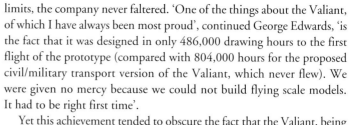

The first production Valiant (WP206) to join the RAF takes off from Wittering at the start of Operation *Too Right* on 5 September 1955. Early Valiant B 1s were delivered in the standard RAF lightweight matt aluminium 'high-speed silver' finish

Ten Valiant B 1s of No 138 Sqn are seen here lined up prior to performing a formation flypast over the 1955 Farnborough airshow (*National Aerospace Library*)

limits, the company never faltered. 'One of the things about the Valiant, of which I have always been most proud', continued George Edwards, 'is the fact that it was designed in only 486,000 drawing hours to the first flight of the prototype (compared with 804,000 hours for the proposed civil/military transport version of the Valiant, which never flew). We were given no mercy because we could not build flying scale models. It had to be right first time'.

Yet this achievement tended to obscure the fact that the Valiant, being the first V-bomber, had to solve many of Avro's and Handley Page's problems too. The Avro 698 and HP 80 were always regarded as terribly advanced, and likely to encounter all sorts of difficulties, whereas the Valiant had to live with the label of being 'simple' and 'easy' because it was ordered off the drawing board and met its timescale. This was very unfair.

The top speed of the Valiant, for instance, was Mach 0.86, its maximum cruising speed was Mach 0.82, it could reach 46,000 ft on a typical sortie and it had a range without underwing tanks of around 3350 nautical miles, assuming that it had dropped its 10,000-lb bomb at the halfway point. All this was very impressive given that the top speed of the sleek Canberra B 2 was Mach 0.84, and the Valiant was three times as heavy. Consequently, it was at Weybridge that much of the high-speed, high-level technology that is nowadays taken for granted was initially tested. Overall, the effort Vickers had to put into the Valiant was probably not much less than that needed to produce the first Vulcans or Victors. And, in the process, Vickers took much of the pressure off Avro and Handley Page.

Once the production line was up and running, Valiants rolled out of Weybridge at the rate of one per week, and all delivery dates from the sixth aircraft onwards were met or even improved upon. On 1 March 1954, authority had been given to open up Gaydon, in Warwickshire, as the base for No 232 Operational Conversion Unit (OCU), where the first purely RAF flying on Valiants was to be done. There was much debate about whether a Valiant OCU or frontline squadron should be established first. In the event, No 138 Sqn was formed at Gaydon on 1 January 1955 under the command of Wg Cdr Rupert Oakley, who had taken over as RAF liaison officer at Vickers after Sqn Ldr B H D Foster died ejecting from the first prototype.

Following CA Release (release by the Controller, Aircraft, for operational use) that same month, the first Valiant B 1 (WP206) arrived on No 138 Sqn on 8 February 1955, just two months under seven years after Vickers had received its first clearance go ahead with B 9/48. Bomber Command had waited a long time for this moment.

TRAILBLAZER

Valiant B 1 WP206 was joined by WP207 on 19 February 1955, and in April No 138 Sqn got four more B 1s – WP213, WP212, WP211 and WP215, in that order. Rupert Oakley was also given more personnel in the shape of Sqn Ldr Bob Wilson and Flt Lts Burberry, Roy Mather and Ted Flavell as captains, and Flt Lts Arthur Steele and Barney Millett as co-pilots.

No 232 OCU formed nearly two weeks after No 138 Sqn on 21 February 1955. The second course to pass through the Valiant OCU consisted of the nucleus of No 543 Sqn, which re-formed at Gaydon on 1 April 1955. This unit was officially described in its Operational Record Book (ORB) as 'part of the Main Force Bomber Command Strategic Reconnaissance Photographic Wing', and it might seem strange that a strategic reconnaissance unit should enjoy such a high priority. However, it was a measure of the importance that Bomber Command attached to pre- and post-strike reconnaissance that B(PR) 1 Valiants with extra fuel tankage were slotted into the Weybridge line early in the production sequence. The intention was that B(PR) 1s would fly high above the enemy defences, like the PR Spitfires and Mosquitoes of ten years earlier, carrying out radar reconnaissance or photography with any combination of up to 12 cameras (optimised for day, night or survey operations) carried in a removable bomb-bay crate. The normal bomb doors were removed and replaced by ones with electrically-operated camera shutters and sliding windows, six on the port side and five on the starboard.

The first B(PR) 1, WP205, flew on 8 October 1954. Ten more were modified for delivery to No 543 Sqn, which was commanded by the diminutive Wg Cdr R E 'Tich' Havercroft, a former World War 2 Spitfire ace and wingman to Robert Stanford Tuck. Shortly afterwards, as the RAF was ordering Valiant B(K) 1 flight refuelling tankers, it was decided that some of these should have dual PR capability as B(PR)K 1s. The first, WZ376, flew on 15 November 1956, to be followed by WZ380, WZ382 and WZ389-399. However, in the end only the Valiants of No 543 Sqn were to operate in the PR role.

On 6 July No 138 Sqn moved to Wittering, near Stamford, only to lose its first Valiant three weeks later. At 0917 hrs on 29 July, Sqn Ldr E R Chalk and his crew – Flt Lt A G Allen, (the squadron engineering officer who was acting as co-pilot), Flg Off T S Corkin (Nav) and Plt Off A R Lyons (Sig) – took off on a cross-country flight as part of proving trials of the Avon engines. Soon after getting airborne WP222 went into a left-hand descending turn, which continued through 300 degrees until the aircraft hit the ground at an estimated speed of 300 knots. The flight had lasted just three minutes, and although the door was jettisoned in the turn, only Plt Off Lyons managed to bail out, and he did not survive.

The subsequent inquiry concluded that the accident 'was due to the aileron trim tab being in the fully up position, and that this was caused by a runaway actuator'. It recommended that the aileron trim tab setting

In September 1955 WP206 and WP207 of No 138 Sqn undertook 'a proving flight of two aircraft to the Far East' in Operation *Too Right* (*David Sykes*)

A head for heights was required when fitting or removing intake covers for the Valiant's Avon RA 28 engines. No 138 Sqn personnel were photographed performing this awkward task on WP207 during *Too Right* (*David Sykes*)

should be limited so that, when using the powered flying controls, the jet could be controlled up to its maximum design speed. The loss of WP222 also revealed the difficulty faced by the crew in abandoning a Valiant in an unusual attitude.

Once No 138 Sqn was established at Wittering, it was tasked 'to provide a proving flight of two aircraft to the Far East'. Known as Operation *Too Right*, it involved Valiants WP206 and WP207, captained by Sqn Ldr R G Wilson (OC A Flight) and Flt Lt Roy Mather. They were accompanied to New Zealand by Commander-in-Chief (C-in-C) Bomber Command, Air Marshal (AM) Sir George Mills, who, with Lady Mills, flew out in a VIP Hastings. The 'flying circus' was completed by four other Hastings, which carried the ground support crews. The Valiants left Wittering on 5 September 1955 for the first leg to Habbaniya, in Iraq. The slower Hastings had gone ahead, and among those on board was David Sykes, a Corporal Instrument specialist;

'At Habbaniya we were waiting for the Valiants to arrive when suddenly we saw WP206 streaking overhead, at high altitude, in the process of breaking the London to Baghdad record. After both aircraft had landed and parked, we placed bungs in the various intakes and replenished and serviced them ready for the next stage of the trip. Whilst this was happening, a violent sandstorm blew across this desert airfield but, fortunately, it was just as we had completed our tasks. When the Valiants left for Karachi at about 0100 hrs, followed closely by we tired individuals in our Hastings, all was remarkably calm.

'After we had been sitting sleeplessly for some time in our noisy aircraft, our captain reported that WP207 was back at Habbaniya with pressurisation failure and WP206 had made an emergency landing at RAF Sharjah, in Trucial Oman, with a disintegrated engine. We then diverted to Sharjah and off-loaded the engine fitters and a spare engine, before flying back to Habbaniya to sort out WP207. When we arrived at Habbaniya we found that the "snag" had already been fixed by the crew chief, the fault being due to sand in the combined valve unit, most likely caused by the sandstorm. After seeing WP207 off, again at about 0100 hrs, we once more piled on board our Hastings, en route for Sharjah, and with little prospect of sleeping due to the excessively noisy aircraft. We arrived about dawn after two days and nights of almost no sleep.

'The Valiant was a superb aircraft on which to change an engine as no crane was needed. The engine was lowered on winches, which were mounted on a flat beam on the mainplane. After successfully changing the engine, the aircraft was painfully and repeatedly refuelled by a group of excitable natives from a three-wheeled bowser, which was similar in size to a ride-on mower. It was then realised that we had no 112V starter set, so every available battery was snatched from the small fleet of MT vehicles and any other sources until we had 112 volts to start the engine! After an agonising mis-start, we managed to get the Valiant started on one engine, from which the other three engines were serially started. After engine test runs, WP206 took off from the Sharjah runway, which was appreciably shorter than that recommended in the Operation Manual.'

The Valiants flew thence to Maripur, near Karachi, Negombo in Ceylon, Changi in Singapore and then on to Darwin, which WP207 reached on 10 September, two days ahead of the delayed WP206. Both jets performed flying displays in Sydney, Melbourne, Canberra, Hobart and Adelaide, before arriving at Harewood Airport, Christchurch, on 19 September. After displaying over Christchurch and Wellington, it was back via Amberley, near Brisbane, Singapore, Negombo, Karachi and Abu Sueir, in Egypt. On 6 October WP206 flew directly to Wittering, but WP207 developed a fault in the fuel transfer feed and had to divert to El Adem, in Libya, arriving back at base three hours after WP206.

Valiants initially carried Gee-H radio navigation equipment, but aids such as this that were dependent on ground beacons would be of little use on long-range flights to the USSR because of their limited range. Ground stations could also be jammed or corrupted, so the Valiants were to be the first operational aircraft to be fitted with self-contained navigation equipment known as Green Satin. This system utilised the Doppler principle to provide a continuous indication of the jet's true groundspeed and drift. This in turn was fed into a Ground Position Indicator (GPI) computer that continuously displayed on counters the aircraft's position in latitude and longitude. During *Too Right*, Green Satin 'broke' after 53 hours' flying on WP206, but on WP207 it 'behaved magnificently throughout the flight', as did the STR18B2 radio equipment.

The post-operation report concluded that the Valiant was 'capable of flying to a high intensity in a variety of climates without the immediate backing of a static base', and that operations away from the UK were 'an essential part of the V-force aircrew's education'. *Too Right* gave the Valiants a good workout.

Within Bomber Command, No 3 Group would look after the Victors' and Valiants' Midlands and East Anglian airfields. AM Sir Harry Broadhurst took over as C-in-C Bomber Command from Sir George Mills on 22 January 1956. No 3 Group already had the Valiant OCU and Nos 138 and 543 Sqns, but 'Broady' was unhappy that a bomber crew could still take up to six hours before getting airborne.

In the quick-reaction fighter world, a pilot often had to takeoff with no briefing time at all because the nuclear age made a leisurely response a thing of the past. Sir Harry regarded Bomber Command as 'still back in the Second World War', and his first priority was to change the whole mental approach of his Command to bring it in line with the jet age, and the atomic bomb. He knew that he could not sell his new philosophy single-handedly, 'so I decided to put a jerk into Bomber Command by bringing in a few fighter people like myself'. 'Broady' gave command of No 3 Group to Air Vice-Marshal (AVM) Kenneth 'Bing' Cross, a veteran Fighter Command pilot who had seen action throughout World War 2, and was therefore used to working with short reaction times.

Early plans for the Medium Bomber Force (MBF) envisaged it operating from 12 Class 1 airfields, of which six – Gaydon, Wittering,

Wyton, Marham, Honington and Waddington – were virtually complete, and the remaining six (Coningsby, Finningley, Cottesmore, Scampton, Bassingbourn and Watton) were scheduled to be available by the end of 1957. Bassingbourn and Watton were subsequently dropped off the list to save money. In 1955 Cottesmore was going to be a Valiant station, so 'Broady' gave it to legendary RAF fighter ace Gp Capt J E 'Johnnie' Johnson to command. As it happened, Johnson did the Valiant conversion course only to be told that Cottesmore was now going to get Victors, so he had to convert onto the Victor instead!

Although none of the V-bombers was especially difficult to fly, Bomber Command was very particular about who was allowed to operate them. The Valiant B 1 was cheapest at £295,000 and the Victor B 1 the most expensive at £450,000, but these figures were just for basic airframes minus 'embodiment loan items' such as engines and internal equipment. By comparison, a Lancaster cost £40,000 during World War 2.

If a nuclear war was declared, 'what we have at that moment will be it', said the CO of No 232 OCU at Gaydon. 'We shall get no second chance'. Sqn Ldr F C D Wright, a pilot on the OCU in 1956, said that 'You don't apply to join the V-force, you are picked'. The average age of pilots was about 30. First pilots, who were always captains, had to be rated 'above average', have at least 1750 first-pilot flying hours and previous jet as well as four-engined piston experience, although the latter was considered desirable rather than essential. Co-pilots could get away with 700 first-pilot hours, but generally both pilots were hardened bomber men. It was an old joke in the early days of the Valiant force that you needed 1000 flying hours just to pull the chocks away.

When B Flight of No 138 Sqn was formed in November 1955, Sqn Ldr Peter Clifton was appointed as flight commander. Peter had flown Wellingtons and Halifaxes during World War 2, followed by Canberras with No 18 Sqn post-war. He recalled that 'the Canberra was a tremendous advance over what we had had before, and the Valiant was better still'. Arthur Steele also had a wealth of experience, including operations on Mosquitoes, and he was a flight commander on No 617 Sqn with its Canberra B 2s when he was posted to No 138 Sqn in 1955. He was co-pilot on the Burberry crew until the Chalk crew crashed in WP222, whereupon Arthur was give a crew of his own. 'I found the change to the Valiant quite straightforward', he recounted later, 'primarily because it was a typical Vickers aircraft – pleasant to fly with no oddities in handling. Moving up from the Canberra B 2 to the most potent bomber in the RAF was a natural progression'.

It had long been agreed that all V-bombers would be operated by five-man crews. A bombing team, comprising a pilot and two navigators, was a given, but there was some uncertainty over the other two crew members. The essential composition of a V-bomber crew was settled during the summer of 1953. The two-pilot option was readily adopted because it provided on-the-job training for prospective captains. A meeting held in the Air Ministry on 30 July 1953 decided it was preferable to employ exclusively commissioned personnel wherever the custody and/or delivery of nuclear weapons might be involved.

Ever since 1942 it had been RAF policy on big bombers to have two men to handle navigation and bomb-aiming, and this would continue on the V-force. After some debate, it was decided to adopt the terminology then current within Lincoln crews and to refer to them as the navigator (plotter) and navigator (radar).

The main weapon-aiming and primary fixing aid of the Valiant was to be the Navigation and Bombing System (NBS) Mk 1. Its centrepiece was the H2S Mk 9A radar, developed and produced by EMI to meet a specification that demanded twice the accuracy at twice the height and twice the speed of the wartime H2S Mk IV. Information from the H2S Mk 9A was then fed into the Navigation and Bombing Computer (NBC) Mk 2, built by British Thomson-Houston. Given the age in which it was built, the NBC was an extremely advanced and miniaturised electro-mechanical computer that continuously monitored the position, track and groundspeed of the aircraft from what it saw on the H2S, while steering the jet and releasing the bomb automatically if required.

The NBS was the nerve-centre of the V-bomber weapon system, and because it was such a sophisticated piece of equipment Bomber Command felt that its operators should understand it inside out. The first Nav Radars were men experienced on the H2S IVA of the Lincoln or the APQ-13 of the B-29 Washington, but the RAF soon ran out of these stalwarts and had to start training large numbers of Nav Radars from scratch. Canberra bomb-aimers were a natural source of talent, being accustomed to operating at V-bomber speeds and heights, and if they were 'keen and enthusiastic, above average and recommended by their CO' they found themselves posted to the Bomber Command Bombing School at Lindholme, near Doncaster.

John 'Tiny' Finnis had been a 'radar op' on Lincolns before converting to Canberras, where he used Gee-H for blind bombing up to 45,000 ft and the T2 Mk 14 bombsight for visual bombing. He was an instructor at the start of the Valiant OCU, where there was a high failure rate;

'Even an ex-winner of the RAF's Blind Bombing Competition opted out halfway through the course because the ground school was too intense. The NBS weighed about 1600 lbs divided into 22 separate units, and it was originally intended that Nav Radars should be able to change components in the air. The impracticality of all this was not apparent initially because the first NBS sets were confined to Hastings trials aircraft working out of Defford for the Royal Radar Establishment. When it was later discovered that only ten of the NBS units would be situated in the V-bomber crew compartment, much of the advanced theory disappeared from the course because the Nav Radar couldn't reach half the system.'

The function of the third Valiant back-seater was initially envisaged as being largely confined to the handling of communications, although it was anticipated that he might eventually have to look after Radio Counter Measures (RCM) equipment as well. Serious consideration was given to introducing the term radio officer to distinguish these men from traditional air signallers, and in the autumn of 1954 some thought was given to dispensing with the third back-seater altogether and distributing responsibility for communications among the other crew members. This option was rejected because the design of all three V-bombers had already reached a stage at which any major modification to the layout of the crew compartment would have been inordinately expensive.

George Stratford was a wartime signaller who went into 'Civvy Street', only to rejoin the RAF and serve with Coastal Command. He was

Wg Cdr Rupert Oakley, OC No 138 Sqn, climbs out of a Valiant, watched by Sqn Ldr Ulf Burberry and unknown

selected for the first Valiant OCU course at Gaydon, and on arrival at the OCU 'crews selected themselves in the bar over a few drinks'. In the beginning George only had to operate the long-range Morse and R/T HF radio equipment and advise on the aircraft systems in much the same way as a flight engineer. However, as RAF liaison teams started to work alongside the airframe manufacturers, it became clear that the all-electric V-bombers would need a new breed of men to get the best out of them. So in 1956 the RAF began recruiting for a new specialisation known as the Air Electronics Officer (AEO). The first AEOs were men who had completed the Advanced Signallers' Course, but everyone else, whether new recruit or experienced signaller, had to attend AEO training school, which was initially at Swanton Morley before moving to Hullavington.

Unfortunately, as airborne electronics was very much a thing of the future, no-one had any clear idea of what AEOs might eventually be asked to do, and in view of the hushed talk of wonder equipment to come, AEOs were given a lengthy course often up to degree standard in intensity to prepare them for anything and everything. There was no shortage of applicants, for electronics in the mid-1950s was the field to get into, like computers in the 1970s and IT in the 1990s. Essentially, manual specialisations such as pilot and navigator were portrayed as dying industries. The black box was to be the new deity, and in the promised land of automation the AEO would be king.

However, it was impossible to achieve all-commissioned crews in the beginning. Consequently, some senior NCO air signallers had to be substituted on the early Valiant squadrons. In 1956 Flt Sgt A Van Geersdaele and Sgts E Ravenscroft, J Chivers, J C Pagler, R W G Peck and O M J Kendrick flew as AEOs in No 207 Sqn. No 214 Sqn's early crews included Master Signaller E C Brown and Sgts M J Frost and P G Game. Coincidentally, a scarcity of experienced navigators led to Flt Sgt G W E Foster flying with No 207 Sqn, and Master Navigator C G Ross and Flt Sgts A Hildred, W Kerans and N J Spear joining No 214 Sqn. As late as No 107 Course going through Gaydon in early 1964, the AEO on Sqn Ldr Jerry Price's crew was Sgt 'Smithy' Smith.

The emphasis on experience was essential given the lack of flight simulators and the need to pioneer everything from operating techniques to emergency drills, but it also reflected the uncertainty of the times. Rupert Oakley and No 138 Sqn were more than just the first Valiant crews. In concert with the Bomber Command Development Unit (BCDU), they flew cross-country navigation and bombing exercises to formulate the ground rules for the V-force as a whole. On 13 August 1956 Oakley became the first pilot to land a Valiant in Malta. More crews were soon to follow because the only time Valiants were ever used in anger was not in the nuclear role, but to drop iron bombs during the Suez campaign flying from Malta.

These Valiant B 1s of No 232 OCU were photographed at Gaydon on 20 March 1956

COLOUR PLATES

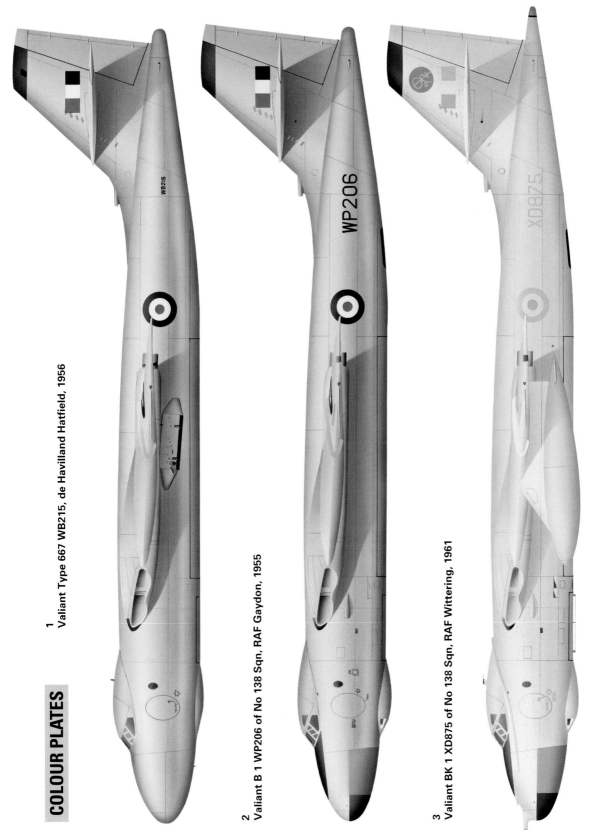

1
Valiant Type 667 WB215, de Havilland Hatfield, 1956

2
Valiant B 1 WP206 of No 138 Sqn, RAF Gaydon, 1955

3
Valiant BK 1 XD875 of No 138 Sqn, RAF Wittering, 1961

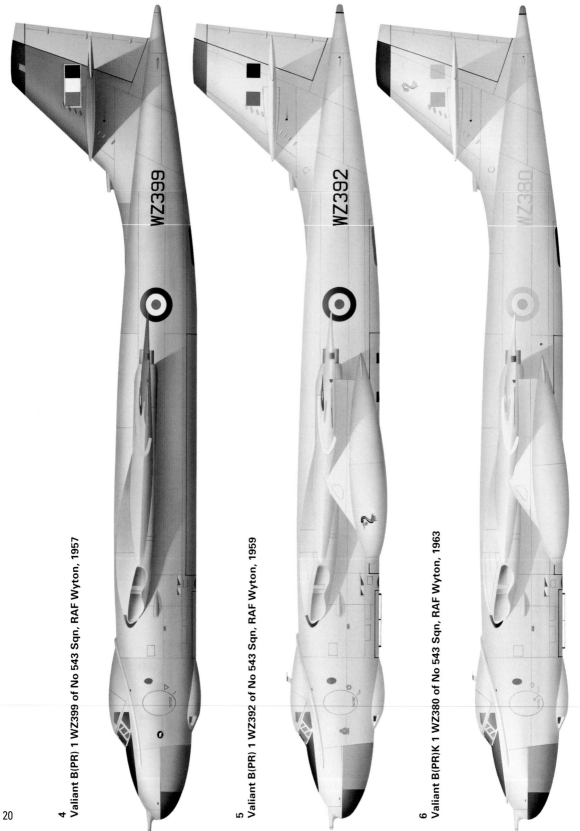

4
Valiant B(PR) 1 WZ399 of No 543 Sqn, RAF Wyton, 1957

5
Valiant B(PR) 1 WZ392 of No 543 Sqn, RAF Wyton, 1959

6
Valiant B(PR)K 1 WZ380 of No 543 Sqn, RAF Wyton, 1963

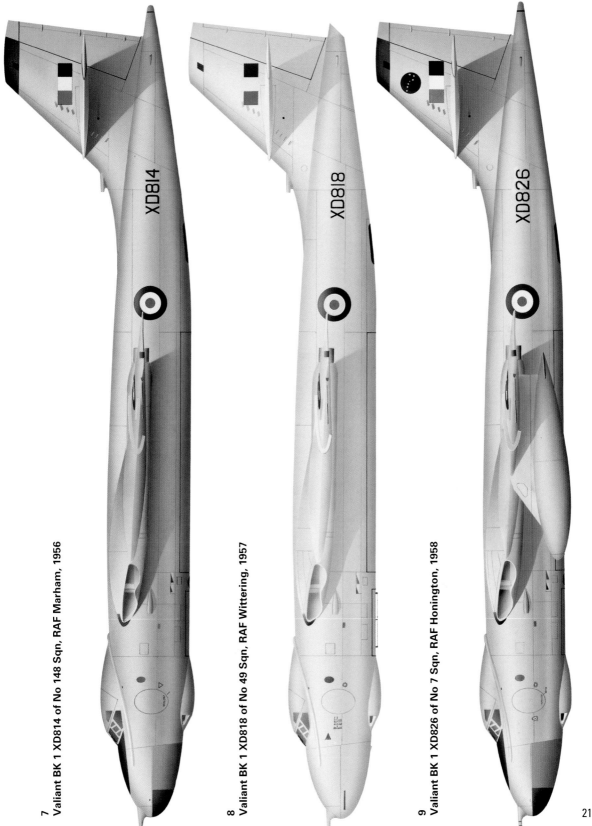

7
Valiant BK 1 XD814 of No 148 Sqn, RAF Marham, 1956

8
Valiant BK 1 XD818 of No 49 Sqn, RAF Wittering, 1957

9
Valiant BK 1 XD826 of No 7 Sqn, RAF Honington, 1958

21

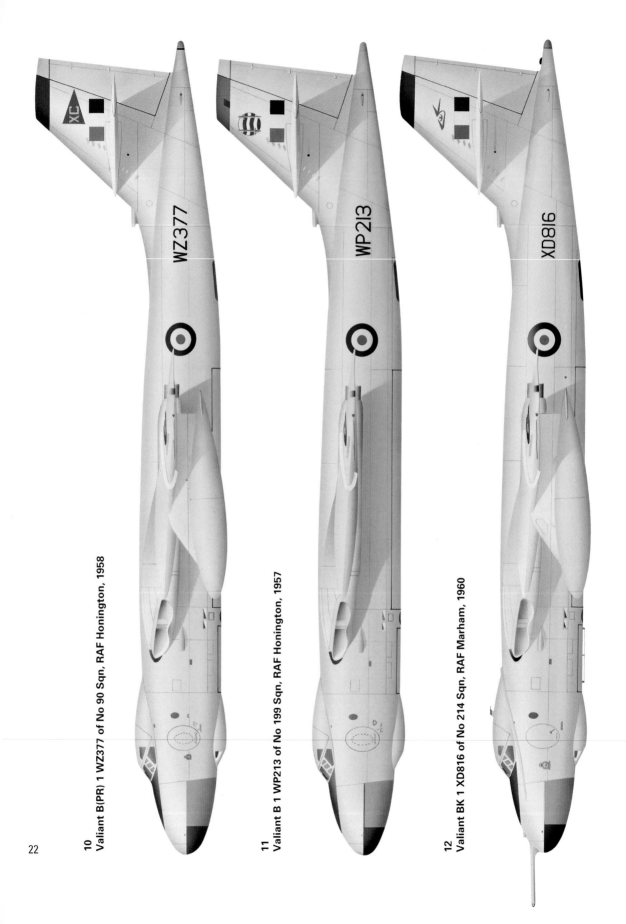

10
Valiant B(PR) 1 WZ377 of No 90 Sqn, RAF Honington, 1958

11
Valiant B 1 WP213 of No 199 Sqn, RAF Honington, 1957

12
Valiant BK 1 XD816 of No 214 Sqn, RAF Marham, 1960

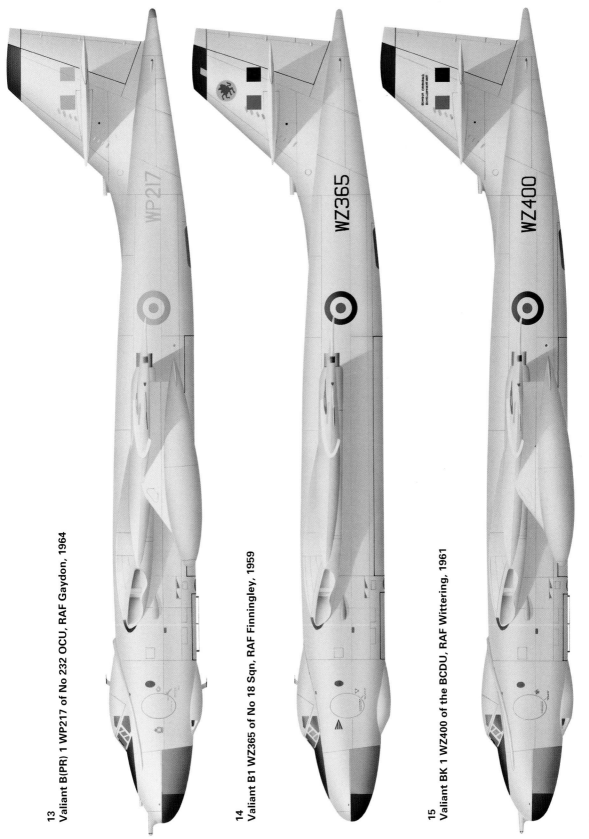

13
Valiant B(PR) 1 WP217 of No 232 OCU, RAF Gaydon, 1964

14
Valiant B1 WZ365 of No 18 Sqn, RAF Finningley, 1959

15
Valiant BK 1 WZ400 of the BCDU, RAF Wittering, 1961

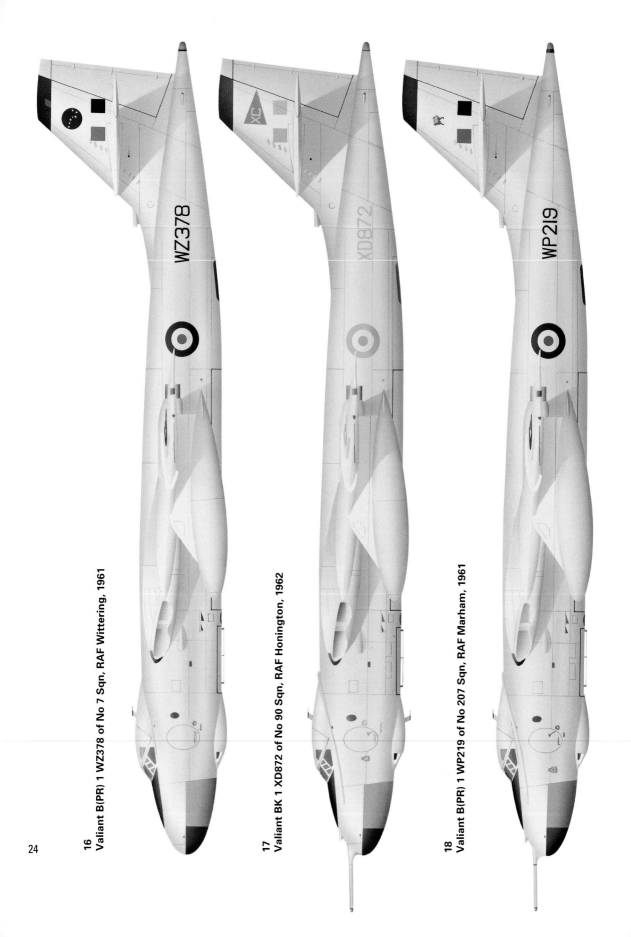

16
Valiant B(PR) 1 WZ378 of No 7 Sqn, RAF Wittering, 1961

17
Valiant BK 1 XD872 of No 90 Sqn, RAF Honington, 1962

18
Valiant B(PR) 1 WP219 of No 207 Sqn, RAF Marham, 1961

19
Valiant B 2 WJ954, Vickers Weybridge, 1953

20
Valiant BK 1 WZ404 of No 207 Sqn, RAF Marham, 1964

21
Valiant BK 1 XD825 of No 49 Sqn, RAF Marham, 1964

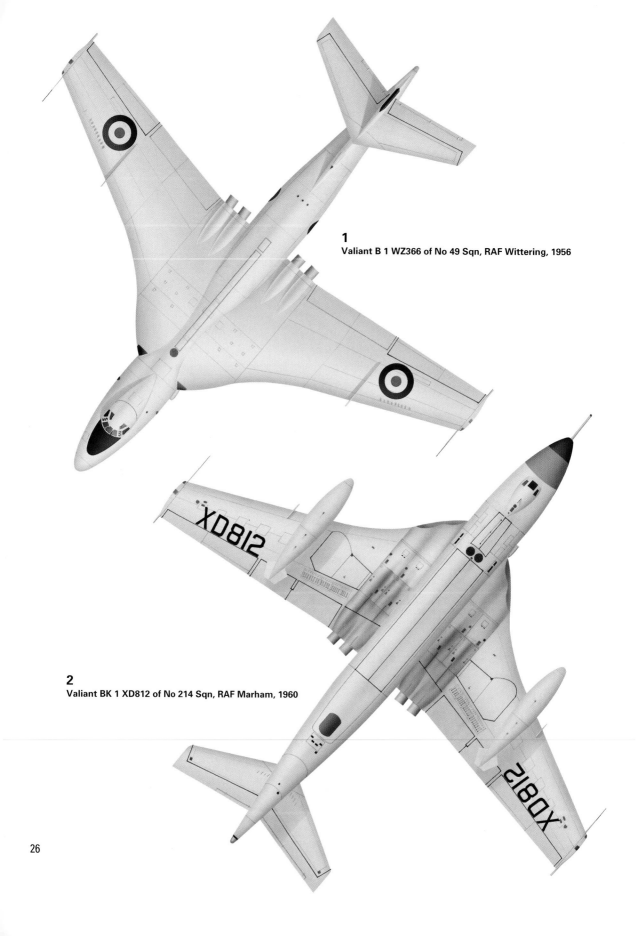

1
Valiant B 1 WZ366 of No 49 Sqn, RAF Wittering, 1956

2
Valiant BK 1 XD812 of No 214 Sqn, RAF Marham, 1960

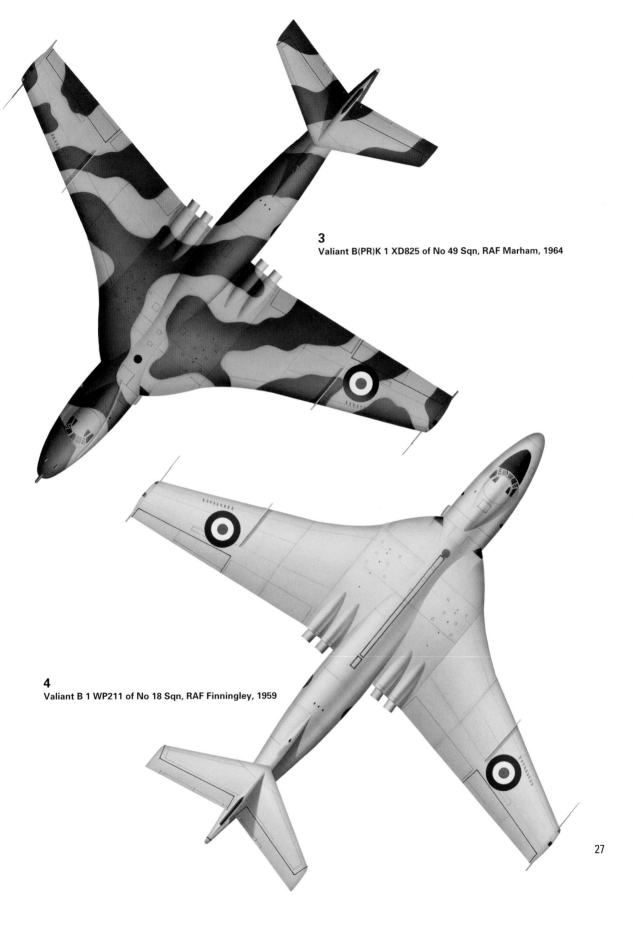

3
Valiant B(PR)K 1 XD825 of No 49 Sqn, RAF Marham, 1964

4
Valiant B 1 WP211 of No 18 Sqn, RAF Finningley, 1959

THE SUEZ CAMPAIGN

During 1956, Nos 214 and 207 Sqns re-formed at Marham, in Norfolk, with OC No 214 Sqn, Wg Cdr L H Trent VC, collecting its first B 1 on 15 March. Two weeks later he and a No 214 Sqn Valiant took part in a formation display to impress Soviet leaders Bulganin and Khrushchev during their visit to the UK. No 207 Sqn was the first Canberra unit to convert to Valiants when it received its first three aircraft in June. No 49 Sqn stood up at Wittering on 1 May 1956, having swapped its Lincolns preparatory to taking part in the first live drop of British atomic bombs. Two more former Lincoln units converted to B 1s before the end of 1956 – No 148 Sqn at Marham on 1 July and No 7 Sqn at Honington, in Suffolk, on 1 November.

No 543 Sqn had its full complement of B(PR) 1s by April 1956, but it was not until then that one of its Valiants began undertaking NBS/H2S clearance trials. The introduction of NBS across the force was delayed, firstly because it was found to be incompatible with the Valiant power supplies, and then because some parts of the bombing circuitry had to be redesigned. It was hard enough designing advanced airframes and sophisticated electronics without doing both in isolation and then trying to cram one into the other so that they mated like a dream. Consequently, the first prototype NBS was only ready for in-service trials in a No 138 Sqn Valiant towards the end of 1955, and even then its computing chain was incomplete, pending the arrival of accurate ballistic information from the No 49 Sqn nuclear bombing trials.

The blank holes facing what the Valiant Pilot's Notes referred to as 'the radar navigator/bomber' were only filled in response to the Suez Crisis, when a panic team at Marham worked round the clock fitting sets into a steady stream of aircraft. It was when NBS was fully operational that bomb-aimers became known as Nav Radars.

No 138 Sqn showed off its B 1s to Prime Minister Anthony Eden on 13 September 1955. Eden had succeeded Winston Churchill five months earlier, and despite his many talents, Eden was scarred by his recollections of appeasement in the 1930s. He likened Egyptian plans to nationalise the Suez Canal to the occupation of the Rhineland, but he reacted with a frenzy that precluded clarity as to the long-term implications of his actions. When CAS Sir Dermot Boyle returned to the Air Ministry the day after Nasser's nationalisation of the Suez Canal Company on 26 July 1956, he opened his address to the air staff with, 'The Prime Minister has gone bananas. He wants us to invade Egypt!'

Philip Goodall was a co-pilot on No 138 Sqn at the time. 'Within a matter of days our pattern of flying changed. As the new NBS was not yet fitted to most aircraft, the Valiants had to be provided with a bomb

Prime Minister Anthony Eden shakes hands with SAC Dick Needham while meeting A Flight of No 138 Sqn at RAF Wittering in 1955

This No 138 Sqn crew bombed at Suez. They are, from left to right, unknown (bomb-aimer), Phillip Goodall (co-pilot), Bob Wilson (captain), unknown (crew chief), Bob Claydon (AEO) and unknown (nav plotter)

aiming capability, [and] they were immediately equipped with a visual bombsight similar to that used in the last war. High altitude visual bombing became the order of the day, dropping practice bombs on every available UK bombing range'.

RAF reinforcements were sent to Malta from September onwards to put pressure on Egypt, with No 214 Sqn Valiants deploying at the beginning of October and then returning to Norfolk. With No 49 Sqn preoccupied with nuclear weapon trials and No 543 Sqn aligned to strategic reconnaissance, the remaining Main Force squadrons – Nos 138, 148, 207 and 214 Sqns – all took part. In addition, there were ten squadrons of Canberras committed to Operation *Musketeer* (the codename for the Suez campaign), four with B 6s and five with B 2s from Malta, plus No 139 Sqn with B 6s operating as target markers from Cyprus.

The Valiant units were sent out to Malta around 19 October. Flg Off R A C Ellicott, compiler of No 214 Sqn's ORB, wrote that 'it is interesting to note that in spite of every endeavour, it was impossible to discover throughout the long period of standby at Marham just who the future enemy was likely to be. Crewroom diplomats and students of Middle East history were of the opinion that Fighter Command and Jordan would be arraigned against Bomber Command and Israel. Other well-informed crew members had little doubt that we were standing by to assist Egypt against Israel. The looks and expressions of surprise can only be imagined when, within two hours of landing at Luqa, all crews gathered in the Bomber Wing Operations briefing room and the curtains were drawn aside to reveal Egyptian airfields as the targets'.

Gp Capt Lewis Hodges, Station Commander at Marham, was no better informed. 'When we were deployed to Malta there was confusion as to objectives. We didn't know until 24 hours before operations commenced whether we were going to bomb Egypt or Israel'.

There were three phases to Operation *Musketeer*. Phase 1 was neutralisation of the Egyptian Air Force (EAF), Phase 2 involved air attacks against key points, designed to reduce the Egyptian will to attack and, finally, Phase 3 was an attack on Port Said, followed by build-up and breakout down the length of the Canal to Suez itself.

As the EAF did not possess any nightfighters, the bombers were to go in under the cover of darkness, but as not all Valiants had yet been fitted with NBS, a radar-equipped jet would lead each attack and drop a red proximity marker on the selected target. No 139 Sqn Canberras would then fly in at low level, using the light from the proximity markers to identify the actual target and drop green target markers to be used as the aiming point for the B 1s. The lead Canberra would direct the main force to drop visually on the green marker. This was not the most accurate way of depositing bombs from 40,000 ft, but there was no other option.

The *Musketeer* plan left much to be desired, as Sir Harry Broadhurst recalled in typically robust fashion;

'I was sent for by the Secretary of State, who asked whether I knew about the plan. I said it wasn't a C-in-C's job to know plans – I merely supplied the bombers. He then said, "But they'll all be shot down won't they?" and I said, "What by?" and he said, "Well the Russians are there, you know – they've got instructors". And I said, "Yes, but they haven't got any nightfighters and we're not going in by day but by night". He then said, "Well, they've got very good radar". And I said, "I know. It was installed by Marconi, and I've had a briefing which said there were no technicians left and no spares. I doubt if the radar will be working".

'He took me across to the blackboard and showed me the plan, and I started to laugh. He said, "What are you laughing at?" "It's a typical Army plan! I reckon you can wipe that lot out with an airborne set-up and good tactical air force support". He then threatened to put me under arrest. Anyway, I rushed out of the room and went along to see CAS and said, "What the hell's going on in this place? He's threatened to put me under arrest". CAS said, "Not to worry, it happens to me before breakfast every morning". When the operation started I asked "Bing" Cross to go to Malta to make sure that there weren't any lunatics out there as well.'

When Israel attacked Egypt at 1600 hrs on 29 October, the solitary Valiant and three crews from the newly forming No 7 Sqn in the UK, together with the OCU, 'were warned to standby for flying duties in connection with operations in Egypt'. No 138 Sqn was the only unit to have its full strength of eight Valiants at Luqa, Nos 148 and 207 Sqns each having six jets at the airfield, and No 214 Sqn only four.

Initial targets were EAF bases that were home to Russian-built Il-28 bombers and MiG-15 fighters, and at dusk on 30 October operations commenced. The ORB for No 148 Sqn noted that it 'became the first V-force squadron to take part in operations by leading the attack against Almaza airfield'. This was made 'by five Valiants of No 148 Sqn and one from No 214 Sqn, four Canberras of No 109 Sqn and three of No 12 Sqn, all operating from Malta. The visual marking was done by Canberras operating from Cyprus. The aiming points were the runway intersections, and crews were briefed to avoid the camp areas. Further instructions were given that bombs were not to be jettisoned "live" in case Egyptian casualties were caused. There was light flak around the target area, but it was well below the attacking aircraft. Intelligence reports stated that there were ten Vampires, ten MiG-15s, ten Il-28s, nine Meteors and 31 twin-engined transports on the airfield'.

The ORBs for Nos 207 and 214 Sqns both referred to Operations *Goldflake* and *Albert* – the former being a deployment to Malta as a measure against a Pearl Harbor-type attack on Cyprus by

Valiant crews being debriefed after bombing targets in Egypt during the Suez campaign

Valiant WZ403 of No 207 Sqn, possibly photographed at Luqa, Malta, during the Suez campaign (*No 207 Sqn Association*)

Egyptian forces, and the latter, sorties against Egyptian targets.

During the afternoon of 31 October, No 138 Sqn crews were briefed to crater runways at Cairo West airfield to prevent Il-28s from getting airborne. Peter Clifton, OC of B Flight, recalled the words of the air commander at the briefing;

'I am waiting for clearance from London to launch you, but if we get the signal to go, there will be no turning back!'

Rupert Oakley led his six Valiants up to 42,000 ft, blithely unaware that Prime Minister Eden was then being told by the US Ambassador that American citizens were being evacuated along the desert road from Cairo to Alexandria. As this road passed very close to Cairo West, the Ambassador hoped that nothing would happen to endanger their safety. Meanwhile, the transmitter on the roof of the British Embassy in Cairo was passing word back to London that 15 US transport aircraft were waiting at Cairo West to evacuate American nationals. Panic gripped Whitehall. 'If you can stop those aeroplanes I'll make you a duke!' Eden is reported to have said to his Secretary of State for War, Antony Head, and frantic W/T messages were despatched via the Cyprus forward relay station to delete Cairo West from the list of targets.

AVM 'Bing' Cross was on the balcony of the Luqa control tower, watching the second wave of Canberras take off, when Bob Hodges got the signal direct from CAS about Cairo West. 'I don't think I have ever seen anybody go down stairs quicker – he went at about four at a time to get the message going'. In Hodges' words, 'as the first wave of Valiants was on its way to Cairo, this created enormous problems because there were five subsequent waves due to take off immediately afterwards. I initiated an immediate recall of the first wave on W/T. In addition, the routeing of the aircraft was very near to El Adem, and they were able to give a verbal instruction by R/T in plain language to recall these aircraft'.

As Philip Goodall recalled, 'nobody had planned recall procedures, so you can imagine the panic! It so happened that the Wittering Station Commander, Gp Capt John Woodroffe, was part of the Operational Planning Team in Cyprus, and he called Rupert Oakley on the radio, "Rupert, it's John here. You've got to turn back". Fortunately, they recognised each others' voices. Peter Clifton saw two Valiants turn back and wondered why. In the end, a political disaster was averted'.

Bob Hodges then faced a situation where the first wave of Valiants was returning to Luqa with full bomb loads and further waves were taking off. 'We had to have the bombs jettisoned, and you can imagine the problems of landing these aircraft, with others taking off, on a single runway'. The five Canberras of Nos 12 and 109 Sqns that had taken off with Oakley's Valiants had been given the new target of Almaza airfield, but when the Valiants took their NBS back with them, the Canberras had to rely on their own navigation kit to position their flares. Subsequently, it was found that Eden's map was out of date, and that the main road to Alexandria had been rebuilt ten miles or so from Cairo West airfield!

Later that evening two Valiant crews, captained by Sqn Ldrs Wilson and Collins, attacked the EAF airfield at Abu Sueir that had played host to the Exercise *Too Right* Valiants barely a year earlier. Philip Goodall was co-pilot on Bob Wilson's Valiant at 42,000 ft. 'As we approached Egypt all looked peaceful. The lights in the towns and cities were glimmering below. Our eyes were searching the skies for any signs of enemy aircraft. The Nav Radar identified the target, and after a steady run he called "Target Indicator away". We turned and prepared to make our attack with live bombs. The sky was illuminated by our red proximity marker.

'Shortly afterwards the Canberra pilot came on the radio with the call "Identified the target". We waited for what seemed like hours but must have been minutes, then the sky was lit up again, but this time by the green marker, followed by instructions from the Canberra pilot – "Bomber Force bomb on the green marker". By this time we were running in for our second attack. All bombs dropped and we turned back towards Malta, followed in turn by the other aircraft in our raid. All appeared to have worked according to plan, and the entire force returned to Luqa some five-and-a-half hours after takeoff.'

Both crews had dropped proximity markers and 11,000 lbs of bombs, and marking and bombing were assessed to be extremely accurate. No EAF fighters or anti-aircraft artillery (AAA) fire were encountered, and attacks continued for the next five days against various targets. All B 1s returned without damage, although AAA was evident at certain targets.

It was indicative of the 'cock-up' nature of the Suez operation that Arthur Steele and his crew found themselves briefly on ops. By the time *Musketeer* commenced, the Steele crew had moved from No 138 Sqn to No 49 Sqn, where they focused on preparing for nuclear weapons tests. Then, from out of the blue, a signal arrived at Wittering ordering five crews to Luqa. They lumbered out to Malta in a Shackleton, only to find on arrival that the request had merely been for 'five aircrew' to man the ops room! However, Rupert Oakley had temporarily lost a No 138 Sqn crews through sickness and the Steele crew took its place. They got airborne, dropped bombs on Cairo West from 40,000 ft and were then sent home. In all, recalled Peter Clifton, Suez was 'a shambles'.

Nos 138, 148 and 207 Sqns left Luqa to return home on 7 November. As a precaution against renewed activity, 20 Valiants and 24 Canberras continued to be held at various states of readiness in the UK.

The official *Musketeer* report covering 31 October to 5 November listed 24 Valiants operating out of Luqa, a further 29 Canberras based at Luqa and Hal Far, in Malta, and 59 Canberras flying from Nicosia, in Cyprus. During six days of operations, 259 sorties were flown (including 131 from Malta), with 1962 bombs – mostly 'thousand pounders' – dropped. Eighteen raids were made on 13 targets including Abu Sueir, Almaza, Cairo West, Fayid, Kabrit, Kasfareet and Luxor airfields, together with Almaza and Huckstep barracks, El Agami Island (where a submarine repair depot was believed to be located) and Nifisha marshalling yards. Weather conditions were excellent throughout. One report written subsequently commented 'the operations over Egypt met little opposition and the targets bombed were large and distinctive'.

At 1645 hrs on 3 November, seven Valiants and 13 Canberras met the heaviest barrage of AAA of the campaign when they struck the radar and coastal gun emplacements at El Agami island, but it was no more accurate than on any other occasion, and no bombers were damaged.

Suez did little to enhance the prestige of the British bomber force. By the time a ceasefire came into effect on the sixth day, three of the seven main EAF airfields were still fully serviceable, another had had its takeoff run only partly reduced and a fifth needed just three craters to be filled in order to be fully serviceable once again. Ironically, the only airfield out of action was Cairo West, and the Egyptians did that themselves by exploding demolition charges on the runway to prevent Anglo-French landings at the base. Subsequent research showed that the 942 tons of bombs dropped by the Air Task Force during the campaign would have been insufficient to neutralise one airfield, let alone seven. Most of the destruction inflicted on the EAF was credited to ground forces.

For bombing, the Valiants relied on NBS/Gee-H and the T2 visual bombsight, the *Musketeer* report stating 'of these, the NBS initially had a fairly high unserviceability rate mainly due to the difficulties of servicing new equipment away from home, although it later improved. Gee-H could not be used as there were no beacons in the area. Thus crews were reduced to visual bombing target indicators in good weather only, with in the case of Valiants fixed sighting angles at all heights'. For navigation, crews used NBS, Green Satin/GPI Mk 4, VHF, ILS and a periscopic sextant. 'Valiants were capable of accurate navigation with Green Satin when sea states were suitable and when NBS was serviceable, and of accurate timing by monitoring Green Satin by astro', the report noted.

'In July 1956 Bomber Command was ill-prepared to undertake a *Musketeer*-type operation', the report concluded bluntly. 'The Command was geared to a 'radar' war in Western Europe and was not constituted, nor organised, for major overseas operations. The majority of the Valiant Force had neither NBS nor visual bombsights, and were not cleared for HE stores'. The report recommended that 'if "limited war" bomber operations are again to be mounted, it is considered essential that the force should have an all-weather bombing and navigation capability'.

Suez at least provided an opportunity to demonstrate the effective use of the new Valiant NBS radar. Sir Harry Broadhurst recalled an alert Nav Radar at night over the Mediterranean 'taking a photograph of something unusual on his radar 'scope, and it happened to be the US Navy's Sixth Fleet. I sent a copy to my opposite number at Strategic Air Command [Gen Curtis LeMay] and he took great delight in showing it to the US Navy, who refused to believe it. So at the end of the operation we left a few Valiants in Malta and took up British and US naval personnel to show them what could be seen at sea by radar at night'.

In 38 years of operational service, the V-force dropped bombs for real only twice – from Vulcans on the Falklands and from Valiants at Suez. But stirring though both campaigns were, they were peripheral to the *raison d'etre* of the V-bombers. In a brooding overview on the lessons of Suez during his last days as Prime Minister, Anthony Eden concluded that the UK needed 'a smaller force that is more mobile and more modern in its equipment'. However, his main observation was that 'it is of the first importance to maintain deterrent power, which means the ability to deliver a destructive weapon, atomic or hydrogen, on the target'. And the proving of that nuclear weaponry was about to begin.

NUCLEAR TRIALS

The initial order for 19 Blue Danube atom bombs called for a yield of 10 kilotons (KT), and by 1954 this had been raised to 16 KT 'by means of improvement in design'. Unfortunately for the UK, on 1 November 1952 the Americans let off the first fusion, or hydrogen, device with a yield of 10.4 megatons (MT) – equivalent to twice the total amount of *all* the explosives used in World War 2. Eniwetok lagoon in the Marshall Islands was lit up by the brightest light ever seen by mankind. Millions of gallons of water turned to steam, and when the vapour cleared the island of Elugelab had disappeared, leaving a crater in the ocean bed a mile wide and two miles deep. The device was about 700 times as powerful as the bomb dropped on Hiroshima.

Blue Danubes were slow to roll off the production line, and by the end of 1954 the stock numbered just five bombs. Being of the 10 KT variety, Blue Danube was assessed by a Working Party on the Operational Use of Atomic Weapons as not being powerful enough to destroy the UK's primary targets in the USSR 'such as airfields or ports with a single bomb'. Scientists and military planners were particularly concerned that the RAF should be capable of immobilising the bases of the Soviet Long Range Air Force. The Working Party stated that 'the possession of a bomb in the 5 and 10 MT range offers this possibility, and would go a long way towards overcoming the need for improved terminal accuracy. A hydrogen bomb to give a yield of 5-10 MT would weigh from 9000-12,000 lbs, and could be carried by the V-Class bombers'.

On 1 March 1954 the US tested an even more powerful thermonuclear weapon in the Marshall Islands, so it was not surprising that on 16 June that same year the British government gave approval 'to initiate a programme for the production of hydrogen bombs'.

As No 138 Sqn settled in at Wittering, a lone Valiant (WP201) stood at the western end of the airfield, 200 yards from the Bomber Command Armament School (BCAS). BCAS was a polite title for an establishment that developed and tested the designs for the British nuclear weapons programme. WP201 was the third production Valiant, and it was flown into Wittering on 15 June 1955 by Sqn Ldr Dave Roberts and his crew – Flt Lts Robert Furze (co-pilot), K L Lewis (nav/bomb-aimer), T E Dunne (nav/plotter) and J H Sheriston (signaller). Dave Roberts had previously flown Canberra B 2s as CO of No 617 Sqn at Binbrook, and after a three-week Valiant conversion course, his crew spent 15 months at Wisley before moving to Wittering to join No 1321 Flight.

It had originally been planned that the nuclear trials would be carried out by the Ministry of Supply, but then it was decided that this could only be undertaken by an operational RAF unit, so No 1321 Flight was established for the purpose.

Nuclear weapons would become known within the RAF as 'special stores', and to add to the air of mystery, WP201 was frequently surrounded by canvas screens. The Valiant stood low off the ground and

Stalwarts of No 1321 Flight, namely (from left to right) Jock Beatie (AEO), Alan Pringle (co-pilot), Dave Roberts (captain), Ted Dunne (nav plotter) and Ken Lewis (nav radar/ bomb-aimer)

its bomb-bay doors opened upwards inside the fuselage on the roll-top desk principle. The smooth green replica bomb casings were loaded upwards from beneath the Valiant – they were filled with telemetric equipment as well as concrete to make them weigh as near to 10,000 lbs as the real thing so that the precise moment of release and trajectory could be recorded.

WP201 carried out the first B (B for ballistics) release from 12,000 ft and 330 knots at the hands of the Roberts crew on 6 July 1955. WP201 was flown on a 'racetrack-like course' to and from the Orfordness range, and Roberts found the jet to be 'a very stable bombing platform'. Blue Danube's ballistics were so good that when released it 'flew' beneath the Valiant's tail area. Strakes had to be fitted to the underside of the fuselage forward of the bomb-bay to disturb the airflow, thus giving the bomb a push downwards.

Up to 25 November 1955, nine 10,000-lb stores were flown for the Atomic Weapons Research Establishment and five ballistic stores were dropped for the RAE from standard Valiant B 1s. By the end, the Roberts crew was dropping from 47,000 ft and 184 knots. The inert Blue Danube was thoroughly tested, and Dave Roberts later paid tribute to his 'marvellous groundcrew' led by Chf Tech T Small.

In April 1956, No 1321 Flight was supplemented by two more volunteer crews, captained by Sqn Ldr Ted Flavell and Flt Lt Bob Bates, from Nos 138 and 543 Sqns, respectively. Ken Edmonds was Nav Plotter on the Bates crew, and he was the youngest aircrew member of the V-force in those early days, having moved from PR Canberras at just 21.

No 1321 Flight became C Flight of No 138 Sqn, which in turn became No 49 Sqn on 1 May 1956, 'equipped and manned for work on the F Series Trial [to test internal workings] and trained for a trial codenamed Operation *Grapple*'.

A Bomber Command memo issued on 12 May 1956 stated that live tests overseas would begin with Operation *Mosaic*, involving ground-detonated bursts in the Montebello Islands, off Western Australia, that month. This would be followed by Operation *Buffalo* – an air drop of an atomic weapon at Maralinga, in South Australia. Maralinga is situated on the Nullabor Plain, an area of flat, almost treeless country on the Great Australian Bight coast, with the Victoria Desert to its north. Valiants were to be based at Edinburgh Field, near Adelaide, this new base being funded by the British government as part of its contribution to the support of the tests. *Buffalo* would be followed by *Grapple*, which involved air drops over a target in the Pacific Ocean.

The principal RAF assets involved in these trials were to be No 76 Sqn Canberra B 6s to support *Mosaic*, *Buffalo* and *Grapple*, No 100 Sqn Canberra PR 7s to support *Grapple* only and No 49 Sqn to supply four Valiant B 1s for the 'F series' (UK) trials, two for *Buffalo* and eight (XD818,

XD822, XD823, XD824, XD825, XD827, XD829 and XD857) for *Grapple*. By the end of *Grapple*, the UK expected to have enough information to produce a free-fall H-bomb to be in V-force service by 1959, a megaton warhead for the Blue Steel stand-off missile and a warhead for the Blue Streak ballistic missile.

Modifications to the nuclear-test Valiants included protection for the aircraft and crew, instrumentation for scientific observations and a special scientific weapon switching panel, in place of the standard NBS kit, to be operated by the AEO. It was policy to prepare two Valiants because at one stage it was feared that the number of live drops would be reduced. Thereafter, it was decided to continue with the practice of putting an additional B 1 into the air for live drops to act as a 'Grandstand' aircraft to give crews experience of flash and blast from a thermonuclear weapon.

On 5 August the Flavell and Bates crews in Valiants WZ366 and WZ367 left for Edinburgh Field to participate in *Buffalo*. The man in charge of the operation (involving 1500 personnel) was Sir William Penney. He had the unenviable task of balancing the need for speed – every extra day in the Australian desert added thousands of pounds to the bill – with his duty to the Australian Government, which had been assured that no dangerous degree of radioactivity would fall on even the meanest scrubland homestead. Penney dared not risk losing the use of the £6 million Maralinga range because of fallout, so he had to wait and wait until the winds were just right for the drop.

Nine times he postponed the first explosion, until in the end everyone was in a state of extreme nervous tension. Penney, in his old duffel coat, began to lose weight and became the butt of many an Australian music-hall joke about 'Penney Dreadfuls'. Then at last, after 15 nerve-racking days of postponements, the weather was just right. The first three devices were detonated from towers, but the fourth and biggest impact of them all was made on 11 October when the Flavell crew in WZ366 became the first to drop a British atomic bomb (codenamed *Kite*) from an aircraft. For this achievement Flavell and his bomb-aimer, Flt Lt Eric Stacey, who put the Blue Danube 'within 110 yards of the aiming point', each received the Air Force Cross (AFC).

Flt Lt Bates' crew flew as 'Grandstand', and on their return to Edinburgh Field a request was received from the mayor of Adelaide asking for the two Valiants to do a low pass over the city. As Ken Edmonds recalled, 'we duly obliged with a really low pass – we didn't buy a drink all that night'.

Both Valiants were fitted with cameras in the tail cone and 'bangmeters' designed to detect and measure the yield of atmospheric nuclear detonations. In Ken Edmonds' words, '*Kite* was armed mechanically in flight by

The 'father' of the British atom bomb, Sir William Penney (in dark suit), arrives in Australia for Operation *Buffalo* courtesy of an RAF Hastings. Sir William was one of only two British observers at the atomic bombing of Nagasaki

the dropping crew, using an "In-Flight Loading" (IFL) device. The IFL inserted the radioactive core of the weapon immediately prior to release. One instruction viewed with amusement was that, in the event of the aircraft crashing on takeoff, the aircrew were expected to climb on top of the fuselage, undo the relevant panel, withdraw the IFL and run as fast as possible away from the jet. Although there was no risk of a nuclear explosion, the toxic smoke from the conflagration would have been unpleasant, to say the least. Fortunately, the necessity did not arise'.

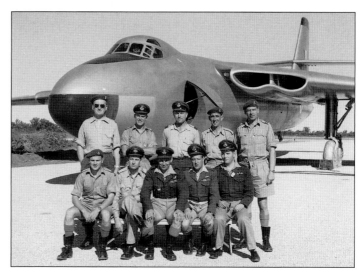

But delivery of a practical Blue Danube was only a dress rehearsal for the *Grapple* trials to be held in the Pacific a year later. The Australians drew the line at hydrogen bombs over the outback, so Shackletons of No 240 Sqn surveyed the Pacific in 1955 and selected Captain Cook's Christmas Island – situated some 4000 miles from Japan, 3000 miles from New Zealand and the American Pacific Coast and 1200 miles from Hawaii – as the best base for the tests. By April 1957 Christmas Island boasted two runways, dispersals, hardstandings and accommodation for 1300 men. The personnel and multitudinous packing cases travelled halfway round the world to descend on a piece of coral whose highest point was only 25 ft above sea level, and which was noted only for its copra and thousands of land crabs. Four No 49 Sqn Valiants came last.

On 1 September 1956, Wg Cdr Ken Hubbard had taken over command of No 49 Sqn. His arrived on the island on 12 March 1957, with the others following. The 'business' part of the weapon was ferried

No 49 Sqn crews pose for an official photograph at Edinburgh Field prior to the first British atomic bomb drop in 1956. In the back row, from left to right, are John 'Tiny' Finnis (bomb-aimer, crew 2), Ken Edmonds (nav plotter, crew 2), Ted Flavell (captain, crew 1), George Ford (AEO, crew 1) and Eric Stacey (bomb-aimer, crew 1). In the front row, from left to right, are John Mitchell (co-pilot, crew 2), Gordon Spencer (nav plotter, crew 1), Frank Coulton, (AEO crew 2), Bob Bates (captain, crew 2) and John Ledger, (co-pilot crew 1)

Valiant B 1s of No 49 Sqn on Christmas Island

out to Christmas Island at the last moment by pre-positioned squadron crews. For each *Grapple* test, individual components were despatched from the UK on two No 49 Sqn Valiants through RCAF Goose Bay, RCAF Namao near Edmonton, Alberta, Offutt AFB, Nebraska, Travis AFB, California, Hickam AFB, Hawaii, and on to Christmas Island. The weapon (be it HE or nuclear) was assembled by scientists on the island.

Replacement crews were pre-positioned by Hastings transports down the route, and when the Valiants came in, they were refuelled and handed over to new crews for the next relay stage. This was how No 49 Sqn's entire aircrew compliment was utilised during each *Grapple*. In early May the Bates crew completed the legs from Goose Bay to Travis AFB, via Namao. On arrival at Travis, Ken Edmonds counted no fewer than 22 fire engines following the Valiant as they taxied to dispersal.

In his 'Interim Progress Report to First Live Drop', Ken Hubbard wrote that 'since weather conditions in the UK had effectively prevented the visual bombing training programme from being completed, there was a preliminary training task to be completed before the squadron was ready to commence scientific drops. The operational drill and flying technique had been perfected in the UK prior to departure. The training programme, which was commenced without delay, was completed by 23 April. During this time 114 100-lb bombs were dropped using the time delay technique to produce overshoot bombing, and the average error from 45,000 ft was 450 yards'.

Valiants XD818 and XD823 were finished in white, highly reflective cellulose anti-flash paint as part of their pre-*Grapple* preparation, and many hours were spent by groundcrews cleaning the jets to produce the anti-flash effect. Final weapon checks were carried out by AWRE personnel, using a test rig that resembled a mobile fish and chip fryer. Consequently, the final checking process was nicknamed 'fish frying'!

The first live drop of a British thermonuclear weapon (known as Short Granite) was made on 15 May 1957 by Valiant XD818, captained by Ken Hubbard, with Bob Beeson as co-pilot, Alan Washbrook (bomb-aimer, and cousin of the Lancashire and England opening batsman Cyril Washbrook), Eric Hood (Nav Plotter) and Ted Laraway (AEO). Ground zero for the burst was some 400 miles south of Christmas Island in the vicinity of the guano-covered Malden Island, and the historic flight to and from Christmas Island lasted 2 hrs 20 min.

XD818 got airborne at 0900 hrs 'V' time and the 'Grandstand' Valiant took off shortly afterwards, making rendezvous at IP (Initial Point) on the bombing line. When XD818 began its initial run, the 'Grandstand' jet positioned itself 2000 ft below and half-a-mile behind. At least three runs were made over the target to check telemetry before the anti-flash screens were in position for the final live run-in. The Task Force Commander gave clearance for the live run, which was made at 45,000 ft. As Green Satin drift was fluctuating badly, the set was put to Memory on an average drift. The bombing run was steady on a course of 203 degrees true and the weapon released at 1036 hrs 'W' time. The co-pilot closed his anti-flash screens at the start of the escape manoeuvre.

This and all subsequent nuclear drops required very precise flying. As much of the AWRE's monitoring telemetry equipment was pointed at a theoretical point in the sky, the Valiant crews were required to put

The crew of XD818 who dropped the first bomb of the *Grapple* series on 15 May 1957. They are, from left to right, Ken Hubbard (captain), Bob Beeson (co-pilot), Ted Larraway (AEO), Eric Hood (nav plotter), Alan Washbrook (bomb-aimer) and Bill Caple (crew chief)

the bomb in a 'box' – a form of three-dimensional bombing requiring not only accurate speed and heading, but also attitude. This was particularly important for the later thermonuclear tests when, to ensure that the explosion took place over the sea, there was a built-in time delay after the bomb-aimer had pressed release with reference to a visual target on the ground.

On an ordinary bombing run it made no difference if the crew overflew their exploding ordnance at 45,000 ft, but thermonuclear weapons were different. The temperature at the point of detonation was measured in millions of degrees Centigrade, so the main method of minimising heat absorption and radiation was to put as great a distance as possible between the aircraft and the bomb at detonation.

As he approached release, Ken Hubbard put XD818 into a slight dive, and immediately after release he rolled into a 60-degree banking turn. In Hubbard's words, 'our *Grapple*-modified aircraft were all fitted with a sensitive accelerometer that measured the positive G pulled in a steep turn. The escape manoeuvre called for a 60-degree banked turn to port, through 130 degrees at a constant measurement on the accelerometer of 1.7 G at 0.76 Mach. This was to be a purely instrument turn by the captain, for on the occasion of the live drop all the cockpit windows would be blacked out by metal shutters'.

When Hubbard finally rolled out on a heading of 073 degrees True, the turn had taken 38 seconds, and as the weapon detonated at 8000 ft, the slant range between XD818 and the air burst was 8.65 nautical miles. The 'Grandstand' aircraft began its escape manoeuvre approximately 11 seconds before the 'bomb gone' signal was given.

What was to become the standard V-bomber escape manoeuvre had been worked out by Vickers Deputy Chief Test Pilot Brian Trubshaw. Too slack a turn was useless, as all anti-flash measures assumed that the jet would be tail-on to the blast, and if the pilot pulled too hard at 45,000 ft he risked a high-speed stall, so Hubbard and his crew deserved their AFCs for being the guinea pigs to prove that the escape manoeuvre worked. As the nuclear cloud mushroomed up behind them, the pilot of the No 100 Sqn Canberra photographing from a safe distance said to Hubbard over the R/T, 'If you do that again, you'll have to marry me!'

The subsequent report stated that, 'Neither crew nor aircraft felt any effect of flash, and the air blast reached the aircraft 2.5 minutes after release – the effect of the blast was to produce a period of five seconds during which slight clear air turbulence was experienced. Six minutes after weapon release, all shutters were removed, and after one orbit to see the mushroom cloud effect, the jet returned to base and landed'.

Seven other aircraft were airborne in the test area – the 'Grandstand' Valiant captained by Sqn Ldr Barney Millett, five air sampler Canberra B 6s of No 76 Sqn and the solitary reconnaissance/meteorological

Canberra PR 7 of No 100 Sqn. XD818, the only surviving Valiant, is now on display in the Cold War Museum at RAF Cosford.

Two days later CAS received a signal from the *Grapple* Task Force Commander which said, 'You will be pleased to know that the air operation went very smoothly and almost exactly according to plan. Both aircrew and ground personnel rose magnificently to the occasion despite very trying conditions. You can be proud of them. I am'. On 20 May, CAS replied that 'reading between the lines – and the code words – I have formed the opinion that probably the first burst has been a success, and consequently great things may flow from it. I realise that technically it was a gamble, but it seems to have come off, which is a feather in the cap for the scientists'. The 'gamble' CAS had in mind was that the *Grapple* trial combined two things – a first thermonuclear burst with a first air drop. Neither the Americans nor Soviets had done this, both having first ground-burst their thermonuclear weapons. Short Granite saw the explosion of a thermonuclear warhead in a Blue Danube bomb case, the ballistic capabilities of which had already been well proved.

That said, the first *Grapple* trial was a disappointment in that the 10,000-lb two-stage weapon exploded with a force of 300 KT, rather than the predicted yield of 1 MT. The RAF lost a Canberra PR 7 over Canada bound for the UK with test samples on 16 May 1957, and there was also a critical situation for Valiant XD822 after the second live drop two weeks later. This was to test the megaton warhead for the Blue Streak ballistic missile, and it fell to Dave Roberts, who by then had dropped more Blue Danube-type 'shapes' than any other captain in the V-force;

'My crew (Alan Pringle (co-pilot), Ted Dunn (Nav Plotter), Ken Lewis (bomb-aimer) and Tam Beattie (AEO)), was detailed to take off at 0900 hrs V on 31 May in XD822 to drop Orange Herald on the target area south of Malden Island. The forecast weather for the target area was one- to two-eighths of cumulus, and wind velocity 090 degrees/20 knots at 45,000 ft – conditions at base fine. In view of this the fuel load was reduced to 5000 gallons in order to give an all-up weight of 99,000 lbs immediately after release of the bomb.

'Initially, all went well. The first run over the target was navigation-type and the weather was found to be as forecast. Then the remaining blackout shutters were fitted, and we went straight round on the initial run, where permission was given to carry on with the live run. The run-up was steady, and the bomb was released at 1044 hrs on heading 202 degrees T, IAS 216, IMN 0.75. After a slight pause I initiated a steep turn to port at 60 degrees bank.

'At this stage the second pilot should have started to call readings on the sensitive accelerometer, but on this occasion he was silent for a few seconds. I looked up and saw that the instrument indicated unity. Experience told me to believe the instrument, so disregarding my senses I increased the backward pressure on the control column. At that instant the second pilot and

This photograph of the first *Grapple* bomb (dropped by Ken Hubbard's crew from XD818) was taken by Jack Bradley, a medical officer on Christmas Island (*Jack Bradley*)

XD822, from which the Roberts crew dropped the second *Grapple* bomb and the Bailey crew dropped Flag Pole 1 in *Grapple 'Z'*

A rare photograph of No 49 Sqn's XD818 in flight over the Pacific Ocean in 1957 during the *Grapple* trials. The last surviving Valiant, this aircraft now resides in the Cold War Museum at RAF Cosford following several decades in the Bomber Command Museum at RAF Hendon (*Murray Duff*)

The crew of XD823, (from left to right) Don Briggs (co-pilot), Wilf Jenkins (bomb aimer), Dave Crowther, Paddy Scanlon, Arthur Steele (captain) and crew chief Roy Quinlan. Don Briggs did three wartime tours as a flight engineer on Lancasters before re-mustering as a pilot in 1945 and subsequently going on to fly all three V-bombers!

I realised that the accelerometer had failed at the time of release. Simultaneously the aircraft stalled, and Ken Lewis, who was making for his seat, returned to the bomb-aimer's well with some force. After regaining control, the manoeuvre was completed in 43 seconds, using the mechanical accelerometer. This instrument might have been referred to earlier had it not been positioned so far from our normal instrument scan.

'At 53 seconds by the navigator's count-down, a bright white flash was seen through chinks in the lockout screens, and the coloured glass in the first pilot's panel was lit up. At 2 min 55 sec after release the blast waves were felt, first a moderate bump followed a second later by a smaller one – the first was direct and the second was the reflection from the earth's surface. I waited a further two minutes before turning to port to allow the crew to see what had happened. The cloud top at this time appeared to be some 10,000 ft above our flight level, and it is a sight which will not easily be forgotten. The symmetry and the colours were most impressive, especially against the dark blue background provided by the sky at that height. As we watched, the upper stem and mushroom head started to glow with a deep peach colour. We then set course for base and landed at 1247 hrs V time. After the training that we had received, this was a routine flight.'

Notwithstanding all the hype about the UK now being a thermonuclear power, Orange Herald was really a large fission bomb that exploded with a force of 720 KT. A giant 0.4 MT atom bomb code-named Green Grass was derived from Orange Herald, and it was deployed in the V-force before a true H-bomb became available.

The third live megaton drop (Purple Granite) was made on 19 June from XD823, flown by Sqn Ldr Arthur Steele and his crew, with Wilf Jenkins as bomb-aimer. The final entry in No 49 Sqn's

No 49 Sqn's *Grapple* co-pilots compare notes in the briefing room. They are, from left to right, Don Briggs, Alan Pringle, Roy Howard and Bob Beeson. Their flying suits show the squadron badge, which was a running greyhound indicting speed. No 49 Sqn's motto was, appropriately, 'Beware of the dog'

ORB for June 1957 stated that 'Operation *Grapple* is now complete, and it can be said that the squadron met its task in every respect. After months of specialised training, the squadron occupied a section of a coral strip in the Pacific and successfully dropped the first three "H" bombs of British design'.

However, Purple Granite only had a 200 KT yield, and a progress meeting held in London on 16 July 1957 concluded that 'whilst *Grapple* had been successful in providing data on the performance of two different types of megaton warhead, it had not provided sufficient data to enable a firm decision to be made regarding the warhead to be chosen for Yellow Sun (the British operational hydrogen bomb). On the evidence of the trials, an interim type warhead (Green Bamboo) had been chosen by the Air Staff, but it was unlikely that any decision regarding the suitability of the Granite-type warhead for a Service megaton weapon could be made for some months yet'.

To facilitate that decision, three further *Grapple* megaton weapon trials were to be mounted – 'X' in October-November 1957, 'Y' in April-May 1958 and 'Z' in August-September 1958. Malden Island was no longer to be used, and from now on the crews aimed for an offshore point southeast of Christmas Island, the bursts occurring at between 6500 ft and 8300 ft.

For *Grapple 'X'*, No 49 Sqn had four Valiants at Christmas Island, plus a fifth that was used as a courier aircraft. Based on the experience gained from the first *Grapple* trial, UK scientists developed a new hydrogen bomb design with a 50 per cent more powerful fission primary stage and a simplified thermonuclear secondary. Known as Round C, this drop was made from Valiant XD825 on 8 November, flown by Barney Millett's crew, with Frank Corduroy as bomb-aimer. While Bob Bates' crew flew 'Grandstand' in Valiant XD827, the *Grapple 'X'* weapon was released visually using a T4 bombsight.

The two-stage thermonuclear bomb exploded with a force of 1.8 MT, which was close to being the real hydrogen bomb Britain craved, but it used a relatively large quantity of (expensive) highly enriched uranium. *Grapple 'X'* was a spectacular success, exceeding the predicted yield of 1 MT by almost 80 per cent, making Britain a true thermonuclear power. As an aside, co-pilot Alan Pringle became the only 'Brit' to have ever dropped two hydrogen bombs.

Derek Tuthill, the Nav Plotter on Barney Millett's crew, had been on A Flight of No 214 Sqn before joining the nuclear trials team. He recalled that in the absence of NBS on its Valiants, No 49 Sqn specialised in long-range navigation training using the radio compass and Green Satin, culminating in visual bombing. Its crew were the elite so far as visual bombing was concerned, with No 49 Sqn enjoying priority access to bombing ranges around the UK. The squadron did not appear to have any war role.

By 28 March 1958, four Valiants and their aircrew and groundcrew had returned to Christmas Island for *Grapple 'Y'* to test a more efficient thermonuclear bomb. On the morning of 28 April the *Grapple 'Y'* weapon was released visually using a T4 bombsight from Valiant XD824, flown by Bob Bates' crew, with 'Tiny' Finnis as bomb-aimer'. The shock wave resulted in severe turbulence and, even with blinds in place and with eyes closed, the flash was clearly discernible inside the cockpit. 'The bomb exploded

at its planned height and position, and the scientific records obtained confirmed that the squadron once again accurately fulfilled its commitments in regard to this operation'. During the post-test celebrations later that night, 'Tiny' Finnis threw the out-of-tune mess piano over the reef, much to the consternation of the NAAFI manager.

At an AWRE meeting on 15 May 1958 it was reported that *Grapple 'Y'* had been a success for two major reasons – the weapons had been 'delivered to the right place and exploded at the correct height, and the measurements obtained were gratifying to AWRE'. This was something of an understatement. *Grapple 'Y'* was the first British weapon to employ the Teller-Ulam design, which made hydrogen fusion possible. Teller-Ulam not only increased the *Grapple 'Y'* yield to 3 MT, making it a true H-bomb by any standards, but also the yield was exactly as predicted, which indicated that its designers were on top of their brief. Only one detonation was carried out during *Grapple 'Y'*, and it was the largest British nuclear test ever conducted. AWRE concluded that 'we are a long way down the road towards achieving a megaton bomb weighing no more than one ton'. The deterrent effect on the Soviet Union of a working British H-bomb went without saying.

During July 1958 four Valiants flew out to Christmas Island for *Grapple 'Z'*, and in August the decision was taken to accelerate the entire dropping programme because international pressure was mounting to ban all atmospheric nuclear testing. *Grapple 'Z'* was designed to develop lighter nuclear warheads, as well as weapons that would not predetonate if exposed to radiation from other nuclear weapons.

As the No 49 Sqn ORB noted, 'The month of September brought to fruition all the training for Operation *Grapple "Z"*, with the dropping of two more nuclear weapons by the squadron'. On 2 September Sqn Ldr Bill Bailey and crew in Valiant XD822 dropped the first device of the series. Known as Flag Pole 1, this weapon was a smaller version of that exploded at *Grapple 'Y'* with a yield of 1.2 MT – it was also the first to be dropped by ground-controlled radar. The 'Grandstand' Valiant, XD818, was flown by Flt Lt Sinclair 'Tiff' O'Connor's crew.

The *Grapple 'X'* crew before deployment to Christmas Island. They are, from left to right, Derek Tuthill (nav plotter), Frank Corduroy (bomb-aimer), Barney Millett (captain), Roy Howard (co-pilot) and John Tuck (AEO). In the event, Roy Howard left the crew for the Valiant captain's course, to be replaced at the last minute by Alan Pringle

On the morning of 28 April 1958, the *Grapple 'Y'* weapon was released visually from Valiant XD824, flown by Bob Bates' crew (with 'Tiny' Finnis as bomb-aimer). With a yield of 3 MT, this H-bomb was the largest British nuclear test ever conducted

On 11 September Flt Lt O'Connor's crew, with John Muston as bomb-aimer, dropped a second nuclear device from Valiant XD827. Known as Halliard 1, it was released on a visual attack, while Sqn Ldr Tony Caillard and crew in XD824 flew as 'Grandstand'. Halliard 1 was an unusual three-stage bomb with two fission components and one thermonuclear component that achieved its predicted yield of 800 KT while being radiologically immune. Sgt Brian Matthews, one of only two SNCO signallers on No 49 Sqn, flew with 'Tiff' O'Connor. 'We tried to drop Halliard 1 by radar', he recalled, 'but the radar packed up and we had to drop visually. We released from 45,000 ft and it took 2.5 minutes till detonation'.

Commenting on the *Grapple 'Z'* bombing results, Ken Hubbard said that 'the bombing task on Christmas Island showed a continued improvement in bombing accuracy, and for the first time a Mk 7 gunlaying radar was used as a blind bombing aid for a thermonuclear drop. The bombing error for the blind drop made by Sqn Ldr Bailey in XD822 was 95 yards, and 260 yards for the visual drop of the second weapon by Flt Lt O'Connor in XD827. Both were excellent results from 46,000 ft'.

During the Christmas Island tests, provision had to be made in case the dropping aircraft crashed on takeoff. Operation *Pied Piper* was designed to evacuate all personnel from the main camp to a safer part of the island, away from the inevitable toxic smoke. Ken Edmonds recalled, during an evacuation rehearsal, the eerie feeling he got being one of only five people left in camp, and the realisation of the implications if ever the plan was implemented.

Immediately after the second *Grapple 'Z'* air drop the Valiants returned to Wittering. Thereafter, the Christmas Island base was gradually reduced to a 'minimum holding state' following a policy decision in mid-1959 that the UK would not carry out any more atmospheric or underwater nuclear tests. HQ Bomber Command directed that from 1 December 1958 No 49 Sqn would revert to the standard bomber role, and all of its aircraft were to be demodified from the *Grapple* standard and refitted with the NBS system. The unit joined the rest of Valiant force in the van of the British strategic defence effort.

Aircraft servicing facilities were rather rudimentary on Christmas Island (*Jack Bradley*)

TRAINING DAYS

A total of 58 Blue Danubes were built, of which 20 were in RAF service by the end of 1957. By the time the last Valiant, XD875, was delivered on 24 September 1957, Vickers had constructed 104 production aircraft. These jets were divided up among the Gaydon OCU, seven bomber units (Nos 49 and 138 Sqns at Wittering, Nos 148, 207 and 214 Sqns at Marham and Nos 7 and 90 Sqns at Honington), No 543 long range SR Sqn at Wyton and a Valiant special squadron, No 199, at Honington. The latter had provided RCM electronic support to Bomber Command's Main Force during 1944-45. It was re-formed in July 1951 as RCM came back into vogue during the Korean War, and the tri-Service RCM board concluded that the most obvious gap was the lack of a centimetric jammer on the soon-to-arrive V-bombers to counter the Air Intercept (AI) radars fitted in Soviet air defence jet fighters.

An Air Ministry Note explained that 'RCM is a means of upsetting those elements of the enemy's defence system that are based on radar or radio devices. Radar detection depends on picking up and isolating a very low-powered signal. RCM, by emitting a large number of random signals over a wide range of frequencies, prevents an accurate bearing being taken on the signal generated by the radar echo, thus seriously embarrassing the defenders. The RCM installation that is planned for the V-bombers consists of a three-fold system to jam both active and passive radar systems, as well as disrupting the enemy communications radio. It will be effective against radar-guided missiles as well as ground radar systems'.

BCDU Valiant WP214 commenced flight-testing the V-force RCM/ECM fit on 27 December 1955. A unique ECM trials aircraft, it had an interesting aerial array somewhat akin to what would appear on the Victor and a huge cooling air intake. The rear fuselage ECM equipment was housed mainly in circular dustbin-like drums, each weighing 200 lbs (91 kg). Vickers designed an overhead monorail with a travelling hoist carrier that enabled the drums to be removed from the aircraft and inserted in a special trolley for maintenance, which was much appreciated by the radio servicing crew.

By October 1957 WP214 was fitted with a passive warning receiver system to warn when an enemy radar locked on and an active tail warning radar in a special radome to warn of an enemy fighter at the rear. It also boasted a Green Palm VHF voice communications jammer, two Blue Diver metric radar jammers for use against ground radars and three Red Shrimp active 'S' and 'X' band jammers and dispensers 'for sowing gravity-launched Window for the confusion of ground radars'. A water-glycol system had been installed to cool the rear fuselage units and a turbo-alternator fitted to provide the AC power necessary to operate the jammers. Finally, five separate set of aerials were located in the nose, tail, wingtips and beneath the fuselage.

WP214 began trialling this lot in the first week of June 1958, and the following month the jet was flown to Canada to test everything over the

AOC No 3 Group, AVM Kenneth 'Bing' Cross, and OC No 207 Sqn, Wg Cdr Dougie Haig, pose in front of Valiant B 1 WZ397 at Marham prior to flying out to take part in the Ghana independence celebrations in March 1957

A close-up of the rear end of a Valiant, showing the Orange Putter tail warning radar dome (which was also fitted to the Canberra B 2)

wide open spaces of North America. Once the glycol cooling system was sorted out and the equipment was found to be satisfactory, the Air Staff gave full authority in 1959 to introduce ECM into the advanced Victor and Vulcan force. Their 240-volt AC electrical system made all this ECM possible, but as Main Force Valiants were stuck with a 112-volt DC system, they would have to make do with the Canberra's Orange Putter tail warning radar and Window dispensers.

Quite separate from WP214 were the RCM Valiants that joined C Flight of No 199 Sqn at Honington in 1957 to work alongside the unit's Canberras. The Signals staff referred to the Valiant-equipped No 199 Sqn as 'a specialist RCM unit whose role is to meet the RCM training requirements of Fighter Command and other formations'. John Godfrey was an electrician on No 199 Sqn in December as the Canberras were withdrawn. 'On the morning of 16 December 1958 six No 199 Sqn Valiants departed from RAF Honington to carry out one of the weekly routine exercises. However, this did not end with the usual return to Suffolk – they landed at a new home, RAF Finningley in South Yorkshire'. The following day No 199 Sqn was renumbered No 18 Sqn.

John Godfrey recalled 'the following seven Valiants were on squadron strength, listed in sequence of delivery after modification by the RAF Watton Central Signals Establishment – WP213, WZ365, WZ372, WP212, WP215, WP216 and WP211. They all had the same equipment installed, with the exception of WZ372, which had some slight changes'.

The standard No 18 Sqn EW fit was a combination of imported US systems and British wartime-era devices – one AN/APR-4 wide (38-1000 MHz) band receiver, one AN/APR-9 wide (1000-10750 MHz) band receiver, six AN/APT-16A centimetric radar jammers, three AN/ALT-7 UHF comms jammers, six Airborne Cigar (ABC) VHF comms jammers, one Carpet 4 spot jammer (400-1400 MHz) and Window.

The ABC transmitters and noise generators were situated in racks in the electrical equipment bay, which was commonly known as the 'organ loft'. The six ABC amplifiers and transmitter controllers were situated in a rack mounted under the pilot's floor in the area normally occupied by the visual bomb aimer. The AN/ALT-7 transmitter, its power supply unit and AN/APR-4 and ALA-2 were installed in a rack to the right of the ABC equipment. The four transmitters, two power supply units and two noise modulators for the AN/APT-16A were installed in a rack situated in the nose radome section. As John Godfrey recalled, 'all Valiants, not just ours, were able to carry and dispense Window via panniers and chutes situated in the forward bomb-bay area. The loading and installation of the panniers was the responsibility of the aircraft electrical fitters'.

The only significant external differences between a standard Valiant B 1 and a No 18 Sqn aircraft was that the latter rarely carried

underwing tanks and had the windows of the visual bomb aiming station blanked off. The standard main force Valiant rear crew consisted of a Nav Radar, Nav Plotter and an AEO, but as two transmitters took over the space of NBS equipment on No 18 Sqn aircraft, there was no role for a Nav Radar. These jamming aircraft, therefore, flew with one nav, an AEO and a special operator (usually a SNCO AEOp, although there was one Master AEOp, 'Curly' Emeny). AEOs and AEOps were interchangeable, and most of them swapped seats on a trip-by-trip basis.

Tony Cunnane joined No 18 Sqn as an AEO in 1960. 'Some ECM equipment was stashed in the forward bomb-aimer's position, but most was in the "organ loft" [the servicing bay], which was accessed by steep, narrow steps up behind the nose-wheel bay. One of the bomb-bay doors was electrically permanently isolated because certain VHF ECM aerials were mounted on its outer surface – there was nowhere else to put them! No 18 Sqn Valiants had a much-modified electrical system because when all the ECM gear was switched on, there was insufficient power to operate them all. In the event of engine failure in flight, the AEO came into his own to initiate a rapid load-shedding procedure to ensure that sufficient electrical power was maintained to the powered flying controls.

'We were a training squadron and didn't have a war role. I think it is true to say that the majority of our aircrew thought that No 18 Sqn's peacetime training role was rather specious – and boring! We spent most of our flying time coming in at high level (above 40,000 ft) from the near Continent towards the UK's east coast, which is what, presumably, the planners of the day thought the Soviet Air Force would do in the event of a pre-emptive strike. At various points we would switch on our ancient jamming equipment with the object of "blinding" UK air defence (AD) radars and rendering their voice frequencies useless due to loud noises. Each of our jamming systems operated on a single frequency so the groundcrew had to programme each transmitter in advance, which meant that the AEO only had to switch the equipment on and off.

'Having a fairly high-power output fed into rather primitive wide-angle antennae, our transmitters did tend to have what were known in the trade as "side-lobes", where energy went out on frequencies well away from the intended one. We did, on a number of occasions, manage to blot out the domestic television transmitters in large parts of the UK, but that was accidental, not deliberate. After that had happened, the inevitable stories in the newspapers and on TV merely blamed the loss of pictures on 'abnormal atmospheric conditions'.

'Our voice jamming equipment operated on specific frequencies, but we could listen in on the frequencies that the ground controllers were using to control the fighter aircraft. For reasons of flight safety, we had to ensure that we didn't jam any operational frequencies. The fighters were allowed to ask their ground controller to switch channels if our jamming affected their reception, which sort of negated the purpose of the exercise, especially if we heard the request and the new frequency was one that we could jam too.

'Quite often it happened that some fighters changed to the new frequency whilst others did not because they had not heard the order. Thus, on many occasions, mayhem resulted, but not for long – our jamming runs rarely exceed about 20 minutes. In any case, there was a master safety frequency which ground controllers could use to order us to switch off all our jamming transmitters.'

On 25 September 1959, OC No 18 Sqn (Wg Cdr D J Roe) told HQ Bomber Command, 'The fact that these seven Valiants are non-standard has been partially recognised by certain entries in the Pilots' Notes. However, there has been no official recognition on the technical side, which leads to many difficulties in documentation and servicing, and also in the installation of approved modifications'. Roe finished by writing 'It is strongly recommended that a special type number should be given to the Valiants of No 18 Sqn. This should save time and effort in servicing and maintaining these aircraft, and would lead to greater utilisation'.

Tony Cunnane recalled that 'We were rather surprised when our Squadron Commander informed us one day that he had asked Bomber Command HQ to give the unit a formal war role. We were dismayed when he told us that Command had agreed! From then on No 18 Sqn became part of what was known as the "main force", and we had to react to all of Bomber Command's frequent alert and readiness exercises'.

Once the Valiant proved to be just another aeroplane, Mike Harrington was among the first pilots to go directly onto the force from advanced training. He joined No 199/18 Sqn as a co-pilot, and he recalled that 'we would mingle with the Main Force Valiants and try to jam the warning and fighter control radars'. No 18 Sqn still had no war role at this point, its Valiants not being expected to escort the Main Force to the USSR.

Apart from challenging the UK AD system's Bloodhound Mk 1 surface-to-air missile batteries, No 18 Sqn also detached to Malta, Cyprus and Singapore. As RAF historian Jeff Jefford described it, 'customers ranged from the operators of the radar sites at such exotic locations as Madelena, Mount Olympus, Butterworth and Bukit Gombak, down to the back-seaters of Meteors and Javelins trying to pick out targets on their AI Mks 10, 17 and/or 21'. No 18 Sqn never had more than nine crews, and therefore its Valiants could only be effective on a relatively localised basis. However, when that effort was focused the effect could be devastating. When describing an exercise in 1959 the No 18 Sqn ORB recorded that 'the Type 80 radar at Patrington had been rendered virtually unusable for target allotment and the North Coates' Type 82 search radar was quite unusable'.

A meeting was held at Finningley on 26 February 1960 to investigate the possible re-engineering of the ECM installation on No 18 Sqn Valiants to bring them more into line with the main force. However, once the Mk 2 Vulcans and Victors acquired a comprehensive ECM capability of their own, there was no longer any need for a dedicated Valiant jamming squadron. There was still a requirement for EW training, but the use of Valiants was an uneconomic way of delivering that. The decision to re-vamp the EW training force with No 360 Sqn Canberras led to the disbandment of No 18 Sqn on 31 March 1963.

IMPRESSIONS

Roy Bentley was one of the first Canberra observers to be trained on the NBS from scratch. He soon became an instructor on the OCU, but to

Roy's generation the Valiant was only an overgrown Canberra with more room and pressurisation. However, there were others who waxed far more lyrically about the Valiant, such as C M Lambert, who wrote the following in *Flight* magazine from the Paris airshow in June 1957;

'Glossy white, black-beaked, wing-raked, thunderously quaking with power, a Valiant takes off like a great sea bird. A slow run past, followed by a second – then forward go the throttles, back comes the stick, up goes the nose, back stream dark Avon-trails and up, up, up goes the pride of Bomber Command.'

Valiant aircrew training was based around a six-monthly cycle of Basic Training Requirements (BTRs), which had to be completed by each aircrew member. The pilots had to fly a minimum number of airfield and runway approaches, with some flown asymmetric and others without airbrakes. The Valiant had electro-hydraulically operated flying controls, with automatic and selective manual reversion fitted for all surfaces. Mike Harrington recalled that the Valiant was a lovely aeroplane to fly with the powered flying controls operating, but part of the BTR schedule was to disconnect them and fly the beast manually. 'It was like flying a barn door – very heavy and needing both pilots on the control handwheel. We had to practice manual reversion once a month, but I never heard of the powered controls failing for real'.

For the rear crew, there were navigational exercises with or without various bits of the equipment working, culminating in a variety of simulated bombing attacks on targets around the country. To have some objective means of assessing accuracy, crews operated against Radar Bomb Score Units (RBSUs), which moved around for the sake of variety.

The AEO would call up the RBSU with details of the scheduled attack – for example, a road crossing a stream in hilly country. The Nav Radar switched on a radio tone signal as he approached release point, and when the tone cut off, the RBSU marked the point where the crew would have released their bomb. The RBSU controllers went into their ballistics tables to work out the forward throw – ballistic bombs had a forward throw of around eight miles – and plot the theoretical point of impact. The bombing score was then passed back to the aircraft as a "Delta Hotel" (Direct Hit) or error in terms of bearing and distance in yards.

The Valiant B 1 cockpit layout

There were also training runs through EW ranges, together with a specific number of fighter affiliation exercises with Javelins and Lightnings. Add in the overseas Ranger flights and participation in Group and Command exercises, and an individual Valiant crew member would clock up between 240 and 300 flying hours a year.

The BTR system underpinned the crew Classification Scheme. A Non-Operational crew was expected to attain Combat status within six to eight weeks of arriving on a squadron. Declaration of

Combat status told everyone that the crew was capable of going to war. Combat Star was the next step up, and it was usually attained when the crew satisfactorily completed a full BTR training period – about nine months to a year into the tour. Next came Select, which required BTRs to be completed within more demanding limits. This was unlikely to be achieved until a crew was well into its second year, and sometimes not at all. Top of the bill, and quite rare (perhaps only one per squadron), was Select Star.

Over a six-month classification period, a Combat crew was expected to achieve bombing accuracies to within 650 yards, a Select crew to within 400 yards and a Select Star crew to within 350 yards. Selection to Select Star required the C-in-C's blessing, and Select Star crews were supposed to enjoy perks such as first bite at the overseas Ranger flight list.

Valiants were operated to the end by constituted crews. Working up the Classification scale demanded a team effort, and it was an article of faith that a crew trained together, flew together and, if necessary, died together.

Back in 1955 it had been proposed that Combat and Select crews should do 5¼- and 7¼-year tours respectively, the tours' lengths easing the training commitment while raising the standard in Bomber Command. As more V-bombers entered service, six years tended to be the norm. On the groundcrew side, the Air Ministry considered that there would be no major continuity difficulties, apart from the Service-wide shortage of some skilled trades. However, the complexity of some of the equipment fitted in the bombers would demand a very high standard of ability and training among the tradesmen.

Each Valiant was entrusted to a specific Crew Chief, who travelled with the aircraft whenever it went away for major servicing, and who acted as the sixth member of the crew whenever his bomber landed away

A complete Valiant team of aircrew, groundcrew, support equipment and stores (*National Aerospace Library*)

from base. Yet in spite of this skilled assistance, all aircrew members were required to qualify for servicing certificates so that they could inspect, refuel and turn around their Valiant on their own.

A Valiant crew generally averaged one five-hour training sortie each week, with the rest of their time being taken up with ground training, target study or an air test. The crew of five would meet up some three hours before takeoff at the Operations Block, which in the V-force replaced the squadron crewroom as a self-contained centre for briefing, intelligence and flying clothing. The first hour would be spent preparing charts, checking weather and diversion airfields, booking bombing ranges, calculating takeoff performance and fuel planning. Aviation historian Gordon Swanborough flew a typical Valiant training flight in the early days;

'A minute after takeoff, we glance at the altimeter and see that it is reading 6000 ft. Three minutes later we are at 20,000 ft, still climbing, and less than a quarter-of-an-hour from the time the wheels left the ground we are at 40,000 ft. A little above 40,000 ft we level off into a cruise climb, on course for our target. This cruise climb technique is designed to let the aircraft gain height slowly as the weight decreases with the consumption of fuel. We settle down to a steady cruise at Mach 0.78 and our navigator informs us that our speed over the ground is about 520 mph.

'As this is only a short training mission, our target is approached after about 30 minutes in the cruise climb. The captain levels off as the bomb-aimer moves forward through a folding door into the fairing under the front fuselage. Lying on the couch in this station, the bomb-aimer sights the target, the bomb-bay doors are opened and the Valiant makes a run-in at about Mach 0.9 [Swanborough must have been overcome with excitement because the Valiant's top speed above 35,000 ft with bomb-bay doors open was Mach 0.82, and with them closed, Mach 0.85]. At the launching point, the aircraft banks steeply away because it has been assumed that a nuclear bomb is being dropped on this mission. Eventually we reach an altitude of 50,000 ft at the top of our cruise climb, by which time we are about 70 miles away from home base.

'The Valiant's speed is allowed to fall back to Mach 0.75. The airbrakes beneath each wing, visible to us from inside the aircraft when deployed, are extended to steepen our rate of descent, and we lose height at about 4000 ft a minute. This is quite a lot faster than the fastest of express lifts, but there is none of that "sinking feeling" in the Valiant. The automatic pilot and one of the most modern pieces of equipment in the aircraft, known as the approach coupler [now known as the instrument landing system], bring the Valiant down to 200 ft above the ground in line with the runway. From that point, the captain takes over. He has already lowered the flaps to reduce speed for landing, and as the final approach is made the speed drops back to a mere 100 knots or so. With an almost imperceptible bump, the Valiant finds the runway, the throttles are closed right back and the brakes applied.

'In less than two hours we have covered nearly 1000 miles and reached an altitude higher than any aeroplane flown during World War 2, in a comfortable, warm, pressurised near-silent cabin. The crew climb down, stretch their legs and saunter away to the mess while the Valiant, out of its element now, is towed away to the hangar.'

While original plans envisaged the MBF operating from ten Class 1 airfields, the development of Soviet ballistic missiles made the V-force extremely vulnerable to surprise attack. Dispersal was the obvious answer, but that hinged on the availability of suitable airfields, with facilities and servicing provided at them, and the possible use of overseas bases. RATOG (rocket-assisted take-off gear) was considered for fully laden takeoffs from high altitude airfields, and two Valiants were involved in trials with a de Havilland Super Sprite rocket under each wing. The Air Staff wanted 39 Valiants to be fitted with RATOG because the four Avon engines in the Valiant B 1 pushed out a total of around 40,000 lbs of thrust. However, once 80,000-lb thrust Vulcan and Victor B 2s arrived on the scene, the hair-raising RATOG requirement was curtailed on 23 July 1959.

Forty relatively underpowered Valiants were to have been given water-methanol injection that was designed to restore thrust when taking off from hot and high altitude airfields. Water-methanol from a 145-gallon tank was supplied to each engine by an air turbine-driven pump. At maximum rate of flow, the 'water-meth' lasted for about 45 seconds and delivered an increase in thrust of about 1000 lbs per

A No 214 Sqn Valiant finished in an all-white anti-flash Titanine paint scheme comes in to land at Marham, the bomber's distinctive bicycle undercarriage being clearly visible. Full flap was not lowered until 200-300 ft above touchdown, with the aim of crossing the threshold at 105 knots at weights up to 80,000 lbs. Five knots was added for every 10,000 lbs above that. Unlike the Vulcan and Victor, the Valiant had no tail brake chute

Valiant XD865 of No 90 Sqn has been marked with the unit's 'XC' and green pennant motif on the fin

No 90 Sqn Valiants rest on their pans between sorties at Honington. The unit operated a mixed force of B(K) 1s, B(PR) 1s and B(PR)K 1s from early 1957

A Valiant B 1 with an underslung de Havilland Super Sprite rocket booster engine (*Vickers*)

XD872 powers skyward with Super Sprite assistance during trials in June-July 1957 (*Don Briggs*)

engine. In the end only 20 Valiants were given water-methanol injection, with the rest of the fleet being left to make do.

Operational readiness was to remain a big priority for the air staffs during the formative years of the V-force, especially after Soviet ballistic missiles were based in Czechoslovakia that could reach the UK in just four minutes. To avoid what CAS Lord Tedder described as a potential 'nuclear Pearl Harbor', Bomber Command training, exercises, maintenance, accommodation and hours of duty became geared to getting a fully operational V-bomber off the ground in the minimum time possible to safeguard the nuclear deterrent. In the end there were 36 UK airfields with Operational Readiness Platforms (ORPs) attached at one end of the main runway – nine Class 1 airfields, five dispersals with facilities for four V-bombers and 22 with ORPs and facilities for two.

'Mick' was an exercise to practice alert and arming procedures without aircraft being dispersed, while 'Mayflight' was essentially a pre-planned 'Mick', plus actual dispersal of aircraft. The next stage was 'Micky Finn' – no-notice dispersal of the whole MBF, as distinct from 'Kinsman', which was a squadron dispersal designed to practice day-to-day operating from such a site, which in No 138 Sqn's case was Gaydon.

Armourer Pete Sharp recalled that 'Blue Danube was an enormous weapon to handle, and the Standard Airfield Bomb Transporter was equally at fault. The towing arm was of almost unmanageable proportions and weight, and could only be manhandled for the briefest of intervals. It took considerable effort and a high degree of skill to position the weapon accurately. Also, it was critical to position the aircraft on a sloping pan so that the riggers didn't have to jack the aircraft up. Even then the clearance was only one to five inches between the deflector door hinge line and the top of the weapon'. In other words, Blue Danube was not a weapon that leant itself to ready deployment away from a Valiant main base.

Besides taking part in a major UK air defence exercise such as *Yeoman*, there were preparations for bombing and navigation competitions, plus Lone Ranger and Western Ranger flights by singleton Valiants – the former eastwards to Wildenrath, Luqa, El Adem, Nairobi, Salisbury or the Persian Gulf, the latter westwards chiefly to the old World War 2 ferry station at Goose Bay, Labrador, and Offutt AFB, Nebraska. The British Isles has profound limitations when it comes to navigational

training because of its relatively small and distinctive shape, and its densely developed interior offered few challenges to an experienced crew. The snow-covered wastes of Canada, on the other hand, being devoid of multitudinous distinctive features to assist the Nav Radar, provided a much more realistic approximation of the USSR.

When it became clear to the Americans that the UK was serious about investing in a strategic nuclear bombing capability, on 1 February 1957 the Eisenhower administration authorised the British CAS to discuss with his USAF opposite number and the Supreme Allied Commander Europe (SACEUR) arrangements 'to furnish the RAF with US atomic bombs in the event of general war, and to coordinate the atomic strike plans of the USAF with the RAF'. American weapons were necessary because of delays in the arrival of sufficient British nuclear bombs to the frontline, and it materialised as Project 'E', which provided US nuclear weapons to SACEUR-assigned Canberra bombers based in the UK and Germany, and also to the V-force.

Once agreement was reached to integrate target planning with SAC, suitable strategic targets were studied and target material and briefing procedures prepared. V-force crews were allotted targets in advance, and the bulk of their training was to be devoted to procedures for attacks on them. The tactics to be employed were dictated by the rigid flight profile of the aircraft, and had to be pre-planned – there was limited potential for tactical Vulcan and Victor routeing, but the Valiant's radius of action allowed practically no flexibility.

For self-protection over 'the vast expanse of enemy territory' the force

XD857 over downtown Melbourne in 1959. This photograph was taken by No 49 Sqn AEO Murray Duff en route to an airshow at RAAF Amberley, Queensland, during an RAF goodwill trip to mark the state's centenary celebrations (*Murray Duff*)

Valiant XD868 of No 138 Sqn shares the ramp at Addis Ababa Bole Airport with an Ethiopian Air Lines DC-6B and a partially obscured Cessna 180 during a 'Lone Ranger' sortie (*Don Briggs*)

had to depend on RCM/ECM. Interception trials between V-bombers and fighters determined the most effective defensive manoeuvres to be used with tail-warning devices. Having V-bombers on stations, however, did not necessarily mean that they were fully operational. In a letter to CAS on 2 June 1958, Sir Harry Broadhurst made the following arresting comment;

'Although we have had V-bombers in the Command for more than three years, it was not until last year that we had a single aeroplane complete to operational standards. We had no groundcrew, aircrew or staff officers with any experience of the equipment, and its associated problems.'

Nonetheless, during the 1959 Defence debate, the Minister of Defence quoted the SAC commander as saying that the V-force 'with its high performance jet aircraft and thermonuclear weapons' had 'an important place in our joint operational plans, which are now fully coordinated'.

As they became 'kissing cousins', SAC invited Bomber Command to enter its annual Strategic Bombing Competition for the first time in October 1957, the event being held that year at Pinecastle AFB, Florida. Three Vulcan and two Valiant crews departed for the sun on 26 September, but it was not to be an auspicious occasion. True, the crews were overwhelmed by American hospitality, and their aircraft were inspected by admiring eyes throughout their stay. RAF personnel lived out in rented houses, and as they drove to work in hired cars under a cloudless Florida sky they could only marvel at American panache, for unlike back home, where everything to do with the V-force was hidden under thick layers of security, the competition scores and latest odds were broadcast daily by the local Orlando radio station!

The British were well fancied to start with, but they were up against hardened B-47 veterans. The Stratojet carried some pretty good equipment too, while NBS was still temperamental. So, out of the 90 crews that took part (making up 45 teams of two aircraft each), the Valiants were placed 27th in the team results for blind bombing and navigation combined. The best British score was achieved by Sqn Ldr Ronald Payne and his No 214 Sqn crew, who achieved the second-best blind bombing score and were placed 11th in the final analysis of the 90 crews taking part.

A Valiant and two Vulcans share the ramp at Pinecastle AFB, Florida, with rows of B-47 Stratojets during the SAC Bombing Competition of October 1957

Prime Minister Harold Macmillan expressed his disappointment with the results, however, commenting 'we do not seem to have done well in the bombing competition in Florida. I remember when we used to take pride in surpassing the Americans in bombing and navigation'. In reply, the Secretary of State for Air said 'I don't think we did at all badly'. The B-47s had been in squadron service for six years, compared with two-and-half for the Valiants, and he concluded that the Bomber Command crews had shown that they could hold their own with the best SAC crews.

The only real downside was the death of Gp Capt John Woodroffe, the man who recalled the first Valiant raid at Suez. He perished on 9 October 1957 while being flown in a B-47 that suffered wing-failure during a practice demonstration flight.

A year later, and with NBS coming on song, two Valiant teams, each with two aircraft and four crews, competed in the B-52 class at the SAC bombing competition at March AFB, California. A total of 41 teams took part in the event, and one Bomber Command team came seventh overall and the other came 20th. Sqn Ldr Richardson of No 148 Sqn came ninth out of 164 individual crews, while the boss of No 138 Sqn, Wg Cdr Sidney Baker, came 12th.

'Is this good?' asked an editorial in the *Boston Herald* on 18 October. 'Well, the British had just four teams and the Americans were on home ground. On each of three nights the crews are sent off on simulated bombing missions. The first target, for instance, was a specific corner of a Butte, Montana, department store. Observers equipped with electronic tracking devices determine the accuracy of the strikes, and other points are added to the score for navigation. It is a terribly exacting test, demanding the utmost in equipment design, crew training and command skill. Targets are a precise point, like the geometric centre of a gasometer in Windsor, Ontario. The RAF more than met the test.'

The Secretary of State for Air was quick to brief the Prime Minister;

'In view of your interest last year, all crews flew the same route, which involved attacking three targets followed by an astro-navigational leg of about 950 miles. We got very good results, and what is particularly encouraging is the marked reduction in the bombing and navigation errors compared with previous competitions. These reductions are doubly pleasing because the conditions under which the competition was flown were much more severe [than in 1957].

'Although they were operating far from their main bases, the unserviceability of the bombing equipment of the Valiants was better than that of any of the American Wings. There was no airframe or engine unserviceability.'

The Prime Minister replied the following day. 'I am delighted. Well done'. His message was passed on to the appreciative Valiant crews.

Gp Capt John Woodroffe, the station commander at Wittering, was killed in a B-47 crash at Pinecastle AFB on 9 October 1957. Very well liked within the V-force community, he is buried in Wittering churchyard. Woodroffe was an ex-Pathfinder, and it was said that he taught Guy Gibson to fly the Mosquito at Woodhall Spa

XD861 took part in the SAC Bombing Competitions of 1957 (with No 138 Sqn) and 1958 (with No 214 Sqn)

VALIANT TANKERS

On 8 January 1954, the Air Staff decided that all Vulcans and Victors should be capable of in-flight refuelling, and that it was 'desirable' that the Valiants should be similarly endowed. But all the Valiants on order were to be issued to frontline units, and it was not until the more advanced Vulcans and Victors came into service that the Vickers bomber could be spared to form tanker squadrons. It was decreed that some Valiant tankers should have a PR capability, and the first of these B(PR)K 1s, WZ376, flew on 15 November 1955.

A paper prepared in 1957 envisaged a total V-bomber strike force of 184 aircraft – 120 Vulcan/Victor B 2s, 40 Vulcan/Victor B 1s and 24 Valiants. No aircraft were included in the plan specifically as tankers. Bombers would be used as necessary, and 'suitably fitted Valiants and Vulcan B 1s could be kept as tankers when they disappear from the frontline'. Out of the 104 production Valiants, it was decided that 42 would become tankers and receivers – 32 sets of tanks for the tanker version were ordered, with delivery by March 1958. Vulcans from the 16th jet onwards would be fitted as receivers, together with all Victors.

In May 1958, an assessment of the V-force made by the Joint Parliamentary Under-Secretary of State for Foreign Affairs said that 'the range of the Valiant, which continues to provide a very powerful element in our V-bomber force, will be increased by refuelling in flight. This is important, not only because it will expose new targets, but also because it will allow the aircraft a wider choice of routes, and so increase the task of the enemy defences. We are now planning refuelling trials with the Vulcan and Victor in the receiver role'.

In January 1958 the Treasury gave approval for Valiant tanker development work to be undertaken on a 'hand-to-mouth' basis until the end of the month. The financiers then decreed that there was only enough funding for 16 Valiant tankers over and above a frontline V-bomber strength of 144 aircraft. It was estimated that these 16 tankers would add some £2.8 million a year to the running costs of the V-force.

Back in late 1955, Valiants WZ376 and WZ390 had been selected to assess Flight Refuelling Ltd's probe and drogue system. Conversion involved the fitment of a probe to the front of the NBS scanner bay, connecting it internally to the aircraft fuel system, and installing a Mk 16 Hose Drum Unit (HDU) internally in the rear of the bomb-bay and a 4500-lb fuel tank immediately forward of it. The HDU control panel was positioned beside the Nav Radar, who duly became the fuel panel operator. External floodlights were fitted to enable flight refuelling at night. These modifications allowed the Valiant tanker to transfer up to 20,000 kg (45,000 lbs) of fuel at just under 2000 kg (4000 lbs) a minute, with a maximum drogue fuel pressure of 50 psi.

No 214 Sqn at Marham was chosen as the first Air-to-Air Refuelling (AAR) unit in the RAF – this was not a popular prospect for a distinguished Main Force bomber outfit. The ORB for December 1957 recorded 'a general reshuffle of aircraft between the flights. B Flight now have all the underwing aircraft and A Flight are preparing to do the initial work converting the whole squadron to the tanker role – a gloomy and unpopular prospect'. In January 1958, Sqn Ldr J H Garstin and his crew were detached to Boscombe Down to gain AAR experience, while three A Flight crews were detached to Flight Refuelling Ltd's Tarrant Rushton base to learn about the equipment that was building up back at Marham.

Valiants XD869 and XD870 sported Mk 16 HDUs by February, although the remaining A Flight aircraft 'are to be equipped as facilities permit'. In February 1958, CA Release was given for both B(K) 1 and B(PR)K 1 Valiants to be used in the day or night tanker role, in the receiver role 'to take on fuel from Valiant tankers by day or night up to the maximum weight of transferable fuel' and in the training role as tanker/receiver for day and night training. All Valiants from the 61st inwards were B(K) 1s. The first 60 included the tanker trials aircraft (WP214), ten B(PR) 1s with dual bomber and photographic capability and 13 B(PR)K 1s with an additional flight refuelling capability.

Trial No 306 was to test aircraft tanker and receiver equipment, and Trial No 306A was to develop rendezvous (RV) procedures and techniques. The ORB entry for March 1958 recorded that 'Phase A of Trial 306 commenced. This involves training A Flight crews in positioning of aircraft and making and maintaining dry contacts by day'. Crews were being trained in both the tanker and receiver roles by Boscombe Down test pilot Sqn Ldr P Bardon and Vickers' deputy chief test pilot, Brian Trubshaw. One of the first recommendations of the trial was to establish a dedicated AAR ground school at Marham.

Sqn Ldr Bardon described the Valiant AAR process as 'little more than the fact that one aircraft has a probe which is poked into a drogue trailed by another aircraft. First, the tanker. The contents of a certain number of the Valiant's normal fuel tanks are made available for transfer to the receiver. When this fuel is not to be transferred, it can still be used in the normal way. In each of these tanks there is an air turbine fuel pump, which takes its air supply from the poor overworked engine compressors. These deliver fuel at the required pressure to the main flight refuelling pump, also air driven, which is part and parcel of the HDU. All that is then required to make a Valiant B 1 into a tanker is to hoist the HDU into the bomb-bay with its fairing, and connect up.

Valiant B(PR)K 1 WZ376 trailing the refuelling hose from the HDU in the bomb-bay

'The hose drum unit consists of 90 ft of flexible hose wound on a rotatable drum. One end is connected to the tanks via the main turbine pump, and the free end is fitted with a coupling and a drogue. The hose drum is coupled to an electric motor through a variable-torque fluid drive coupling. The motor is always attempting to wind the hose in, but by varying the amount of fluid circulating in the coupling (and hence the torque transmitted to the drum), the drag of the hose and drogue can be made to exceed the wind-in load, which will allow the hose to be trailed and stay trailed.

'By balancing the wind-in load against the drag load, the hose drum will then become sensitive to changes in the relative speed of the two aircraft when in contact. If the receiver flies a little faster than the tanker, the pressure of the probe nozzle against the drogue will oppose the drag and the hose will be wound in at the same rate as the overtaking speed. The reverse will apply as the receiver falls back. The hose tension will therefore remain constant throughout the contact.

'The receiver is equipped with a probe attached to the nose of the aircraft, from which a fuel pipe runs around the canopy and into the normal ground refuelling lines. When the probe nozzle enters the coupling at the end of the hose, it is gripped by rollers mounted on spring-loaded toggle arms. The load required to make contact is less than that required to break it, so the chances of an inadvertent disconnect are reduced. Floating valves in the probe and drogue coupling act on each other at the moment of contact, and fuel flows as soon as the main fuel cock in the HDU is opened. This, together with the start up of the main pump, occurs automatically as soon as seven feet of hose is wound in.

'Signalling lights are fitted to the HDU, which enables the operation to be conducted without the use of R/T. An amber light will indicate that contact may be made, and when several feet is wound on the drum, this will change to green, indicating that the fuel cock is opened. A pressure gauge tapped off the flight refuelling lines to the receiver will indicate that fuel is being transferred. The third and last light is a red one, which will indicate that a contact must not be attempted or, if already in contact, it must be broken off without delay.

'The equipment is controlled by an operator [the Nav Radar] seated at a special panel [on the cabin starboard wall]. At this panel he can control the hose and the tank pumps, observe the rate of transfer and monitor the quantity of fuel that has flowed. Panel operation is very straightforward, and only a short course is necessary to understand its mysteries

'Let it be assumed that the tanker is flying in a steady and purposeful straight line, with the drogue trailing peacefully behind, undisturbed either by rough air or random twitchings of the tanker pilot on his controls. Before charging uncouthly into contact, one should examine the tanker to establish first, that it is one of ours and, second, is the particular one briefed. Using someone else's tanker would be on a par with drinking someone else's grog.

'Then it should be noted from the signal lights whether or not the tanker crew are ready for contact. When they are, one can move in directly astern, still keeping the signal lights in view in case somebody changes his mind at the last moment. Twenty to thirty yards behind the drogue is sufficient, and roughly in line with it. It is an advantage to fly for a moment or two at the same speed as the tanker, and note what that speed is. The correct closing speed can then be established. Still watching the signal lights out of the corner of one's eye, apply a small amount of power and allow the aircraft to approach the drogue at certainly not more than five knots closing speed. Try and keep the probe boring remorselessly towards the centre of the drogue, and overcome a tendency of one's limbs to approach a condition of complete rigor mortis.

'When only a few feet from the drogue, the slightest unnecessary movement on the controls is sufficient to send the probe away to one side or the other, or above or below. It is very easy to believe that these spasmodic movements are in fact the drogue thrashing about, and before long one is exhausting one's repertoire of curses on the head of the tanker pilot. When the probe nozzle is really close to the drogue, a dull roaring sound will be heard and a mild buffet felt. This may be ignored, as it is only the drogue trying to produce the amount of drag required from it to balance the HDU motor. But the effect of its turbulent wake will be to reduce the closing speed, so when the nozzle is just outside the drogue periphery, and pointing in the right direction, apply a small amount of power and the probe will sail into the coupling and connect up with a most satisfying *CLUNK*.

If, however, the excitement becomes too great, it is possible (and usual) that at the moment of applying that last little burst of power, one's arm may give an involuntary twitch on the controls. The effect of this is sufficient to deflect the probe so that it misses the drogue altogether, with the result that it looms up outside the cockpit windscreen like some vast speaking trumpet, roaring abuse and jeers.

'When a contact has been made in the prescribed manner, the little burst of power necessary to achieve it should immediately be reduced. Ideally, a distinct pause should be made to enable one's thoughts to be re-orientated, and the urge to shout in triumph suppressed. A little power may then be applied to move under perfect control up into the refuelling position. This is marked quite clearly on the hose by a large yellow band, which should be kept hovering halfway into the HDU. The fuel will now be flowing as indicated on the pressure gauge in the receiver, and it is just a question of sitting there until the transfer is complete. The time that this takes will seem interminable, but provided that no exaggerated control movements are made, and the increase of weight is anticipated early enough on the throttles, station keeping presents no problems.

'If at any time a red light is signalled, an emergency disconnect must be made by closing the throttles. The receiver will then fall back rapidly, and when the hose reaches a speed of five feet a second, a brake on the hose drum will be applied and the contact will be broken. Every effort has been made to ensure that no fuel escapes from the coupling either during the transfer or on breaking contact. In any event, except during an emergency "disconnect", it should be no more than the merest whiff. On an emergency break one may expect a little more.

'The completion of transfer is indicated by the fuel transfer pressure gauge reading zero, by the tanks indicating full and the refuelling valves in the receiver's tanks indicating "closed". As much care should be taken in breaking contact as in making it – emergency breaks throw a heavy strain on the hose and the rest of the equipment. When it is decided to break contact, the throttles should be closed just enough to start the hose slowly unwinding off the drum. By playing it on the throttles, the aircraft should be allowed to fall back slowly to full trail, the last seven feet being indicated by an amber light and a length of gaily striped hose. When the end is reached, the drogue will part from the probe gently and without fuss. If the point of parting is anything other than the natural trailing position of the hose, it will plunge off in that direction with astonishing

The drogue, dubbed the 'jeering trumpet' by RAF pilots

haste. It will then reappear at odd intervals as it roars past the windscreen, and it is as well to keep out of its way.

'The problem of flight refuelling at night has been solved by the simple expedient of making it as bright as day by suitably positioned lights. Receiver pilots can take heart, for the task of making contact is well within everyone's capability, and proficiency can be achieved in a very few trips. It speaks highly of the simplicity of the system.'

In September 1958 No 214 Sqn gave the first public demonstrations of jet AAR during the Farnborough airshow. The unit was still part of the Main Force of Bomber Command, as was shown in September 1958 when one of its Valiants did a 'scramble' takeoff from Marham in three-and-a-half minutes. As Nav Radar Ernie Wallis recalled, 'I joined the Squadron in 1958 when it was divided into a bombing Flight and an AAR Flight. The Tanker Flight proved the probe and drogue system on large aircraft. Tanking was vital for the Lightning, as the F 3 carried so little fuel that it almost had to declare a fuel emergency on takeoff'.

On 6 June 1958, during Exercise *Full Play*, No 214 Sqn was visited by a reporter from *The Times*, who wrote that the V-force 'in some three years of operation have worked up their Valiants into a formidable weapon in their own right, well able to press home their attacks with superb efficiency'. Describing V-force crews as 'the elite of the Service', with salaries in the £1500-2000 a year bracket, the reporter saw them as 'qualified technicians' when 'automation has come to the bombers'.

On a three-hour sorties with Sqn Ldr Furze and his crew – 'a mere 2000-mile trip which covered the English Channel, Devon, Scotland, the tip of Northern Ireland, the Shetlands and the northeast coast' – the correspondent felt that 'there was no sense of flying, simply the subdued hum as in a power station, and three men sitting quietly, two of them watching radar screens and dials which give position, height, speed and courses. Occasionally the aircraft trembles slightly, but there is nothing to indicate movement. Even in the cockpit the bomber seems suspended in space, with hundreds of miles of cloud stretching far away below'.

The writer waxed lyrical about SAC circling the world, 'and it is their proud boast that they have an aircraft in the sky every minute of the day and night. They are the embracing shield of the free world, and if at times they seem fanatical in their approach to ensuring peace, they nevertheless have reached a superb degree of skill. But Bomber Command's V-force – smaller than SAC – is served by men and aircraft who are the equal of any, but who are past masters at the art of hiding lights under bushels'.

Maximum speed for streaming the Valiant hose was 300 knots or Mach 0.8, and the maximum speed for making contact was 250 knots or Mach 0.76. There was no altitude limit. Ernie Wallis recalled that there was an American APN-69 responder beacon available which showed the Nav Radar in the receiver Valiant how far away the tanker was, but this equipment was very expensive, and it was only fitted to tanker trials Valiant B(PR)K 1 WZ390. Until the arrival into service of air-to-air TACAN, 'we joined up by homing to a known point, which was usually on the coast so it stood out on the NBS. There was also a modification on the NBS Radar known as Fishpool, which enabled you to see another Valiant up to seven miles away and below, although you could sometimes see up to 500-1000 ft above with some fiddling'.

In 1959 No 214 Sqn's AAR training and practices finally came good. In January the ORB reported that, 'The first transfers of fuel in the air [wet hook-ups] were carried out by crews captained by Sqn Ldrs J Garstin and S Price and Flt Lt B Fern. Between 26 January and month-end, these crews completed 26 day and 17 night wet hook-ups'. When the February ORB entry stated that, 'the emphasis this month was placed on flight refuelling training and little bombing and navigation was carried out', the writing was on the wall for No 214 Sqn as a bomber unit.

April 1959 – the month in which Treasury approval was given for the establishment of 16 Valiant tankers – saw the first long-distance proving flights for what was still part of Trial 306. As No 214 Sqn's ORB told it, 'Three long-range flight-refuelled flights were carried out this month, two to Embakasi and one to Salisbury, Southern Rhodesia. Sqn Ldr S Price and crew flew to Embakasi on 6 April, followed by Flt Lt B Fern and crew on the 7th. Flt Lt Fern and crew set up an unofficial record for the England-Nairobi flight with a time of 7 hrs 40 min – an average speed of 567 mph. On both the outward and return flights the aircraft was refuelled by No 214 Sqn tankers over Malta.

'For the flight to Salisbury, tankers were based at Idris, in Libya, for the outward flight and at Nairobi and Idris for the return. On 16 April, OC No 214 Sqn, Wg Cdr M J Beetham, and his crew flew from Marham to Salisbury in a record time of 10 hrs 12 min – an average speed of 522 mph. This flight of 5320 miles is the longest non-stop flight yet by an RAF jet. RVs and flight refuelling took place over Idris on the outward flight and over Lake Victoria and Idris on the homeward flight.'

The day before Mike Beetham's flight to Salisbury, a Press conference was held at Marham to explain the purpose of, and the techniques to be used on, the flight to the national and local media. Next day, the hook-up over Idris was filmed from 40,000 ft by a No 58 Sqn PR Canberra out of Wyton, and this footage was shown on television and cinema screens. In *Flight* magazine, Wg Cdr Beetham was quoted as saying, after arriving at Salisbury, that 'the purpose of these flights, which will continue to increase in range, is to perfect operating procedures, especially rendezvous techniques and signals communications'. AOC No 3 Group said that the unit was training to do aerial refuelling in any part of the world. It would be a requirement for fighters such as the Lightning, although at the moment its use was confined to Bomber Command.

Thereafter, No 214 Sqn gradually increased the non-stop distances flown by Valiants to 8000 miles – the distance of a UK-Singapore deployment. On 18 June Mike Beetham and his crew set up an unofficial UK-Johannesburg record, over-flying Jan Smuts airfield 11 hrs 3 min after leaving Marham – a distance of 5845 miles, covered at an average speed of 529 mph.

AVM Micky Dwyer, AOC No 3 Group, briefs Sqn Ldr J H Garstin and his No 214 Sqn crew prior to their 8110-mile flight from Marham to Changi, Singapore, on 25-26 May 1960

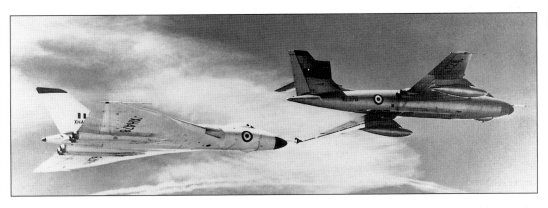

Valiant B(PR)K 1 WZ376 refuels Vulcan B 1 XH478 during trials in 1958-59. The former was one of two Valiants selected to assess Flight Refuelling Ltd's probe and drogue system in late 1955, while XH478 was the test aircraft for the nose-mounted refuelling probe

The squadron's ORB for that month proudly recorded that 'this was the first-ever non-stop flight *to* South Africa, and beat the previous record set up by a de Havilland Comet in 1957 by two hours'. In July, the Beetham crew again went to South Africa, setting up two more unofficial records – flying from overhead London Airport to D F Malan Airport, Capetown, a distance of 6060 miles, in 11 hrs 28 min at an average speed of 530 mph, and returning from D F Malan Airport to overhead London Airport in a time of 12 hrs 20 min at an average speed of 491.5 mph. These times beat the official records held by a Canberra by 53 minutes on the outward flight and 56 minutes on the return flight. On these flights to South Africa and to Southern Rhodesia, refuelling was undertaken over Nigeria by No 214 Sqn tankers based at Kano.

Sixteen Valiant tankers was never going to be enough to support the whole V-bomber force, or to sustain a 24/7 airborne alert posture along SAC lines, but an impressive step-change was made in October 1959 when No 214 Sqn started refuelling practice with Vulcans. On 28 October one of the unit's tankers 'rendezvoused with a Vulcan of No 101 Sqn and a start was made on converting Vulcan crews to the receiver role. Sqn Ldr B E Fern flew as a co-pilot in the Vulcan to check out the pilots. Owing to adverse weather and the unavailability of Vulcan aircraft, no further conversion flights were carried out during the month, but these flights will be resumed in November'. Trial 306A – an evaluation of the Rebecca/Eureka rendezvous aid – and Trial 306B, which evaluated the NBS as a flight-refuelling positioning aid, were undertaken en route.

The No 214 Sqn ORB for November was able to declare that 'with the publication of the Final Report on the Flight Refuelling Trial dated 30 November 1959, Trial 306, which has occupied the major portion of the squadron effort since January 1958, came to an end'. Consequently, from November 1959 the V-force had an operational AAR capability.

No 214 Sqn sent two of its Valiants on a Sunspot detachment to RAF Luqa at the beginning of September, with two more to follow between 16-22 September, for Exercise *Crescent Mace*, when eight successful sorties were flown against the US Navy's Sixth Fleet. The detachment ended on 7 October, and during that month 'the squadron flew 25 flight-refuelling training sorties as part of the programme for the training of new crews and the continuation training of experienced crews. A total of 76 day and 15 night wet contacts were carried out during these sorties. In addition, 15 bombing and cross-country details were carried out as part

63

of the normal unit bombing and classification training'.

The climax of V-force refuelling came on 20/21 June 1961 when a Vulcan B 1A of No 617 Sqn flew non-stop from Scampton to Sydney in 20 hrs 5 min, supported by No 214 Sqn Valiants. The Vulcan was refuelled over Akrotiri, Karachi, Singapore and 500 miles south of Singapore, with nine tankers being involved. Sir Kenneth Cross was now C-in-C Bomber Command, and the operation lived up to his claim that it was 'an advertisement of our deterrent potential'.

'Kissing cousins'. Valiant B(PR)K 1 WZ376 refuels a USAF F-101C Voodoo (almost certainly from the RAF Bentwaters-based 81st Tactical Fighter Wing), again during early tanker flight trials. The Valiant K 1 could not have refuelled a SAC bomber, which employed the flying boom AAR system rather than the hose and drogue

Receiver training for Javelin crews of No 23 Sqn started in June 1960, and four jets were in-flight refuelled from the UK to Butterworth during Operation *Dyke Tankex* during October 1960. In August 1961, Honington-based No 90 Sqn began converting to become the second operational tanker unit. On 1 April 1962, Nos 214 and 90 Sqns officially lost their bomber roles and became dedicated tanker units. Operational training continued with Vulcans of No 50 Sqn, Sea Vixens of 899 Naval Air Squadron, Victors of No 57 Sqn and Lightnings of No 56 Sqn.

Two of the most interesting Valiant AAR exercises were the refuelling of Scimitars from RNAS Lossiemouth to HMS *Ark Royal* 'somewhere in the Mediterranean', and Exercise *Walkabout*, in which three No 101 Sqn Vulcan B 1As flew non-stop from Waddington to Perth, Western Australia, in July 1963. It took 18 hrs 7 min, with 12 Valiants from Nos 90 and 214 Sqns providing fuel over El Adem, Khormaksar and Gan.

The 1961 Defence White Review allocated £0.6 million to converting a third single-point Valiant tanker squadron to provide additional AAR support for the RAF's air transport force, but by this time the operational limitations of the Valiant tanker had become apparent. The jet's small transferable fuel load and single ventral hose required multiple tankers to support even a single fighter on most trail stages. Also, the Valiant tanker was hard pressed to keep up with the most advanced Lightnings, and it would certainly be too slow to refuel the TSR 2. However, the overriding shortcoming was that the Valiant's planned fatigue life ran out in 1968.

The proposed Victor K 1 tanker would be able to transfer an estimated 98,500 lbs of fuel as against 45,000 lbs for the Valiant, and its maximum refuelling height and speed would be 40,000 ft/Mach 0.91, compared to 32,000 ft/Mach 0.74 for the Valiant. The K 1 would also have two wing refuelling points as well as an HDU compared to the Valiant's single HDU. Therefore, unsurprisingly, the Air Council decided on 22 November 1962 that the Victor should replace the Valiant in the tanker role, and that the third tanker unit should be formed with K 1s.

Soon to hand over the AAR baton, WZ376 refuels Victor B 1 XA930

VALIANT AND VIGILANT

The original specification stressed that V-bombers were to be 'for worldwide use in the RAF', and the accompanying operational requirement laid down that the aircraft were to be capable of attacking a target 'from a base which may be anywhere in the world'. A 'bombing-up' demonstration at Wisley in October 1954 showed that the Valiant bomb-bay could accommodate 21 1000-lb MC Mk 6 bombs, or one 10,000-lb HC bomb or ten 2000-lb Mk 9 mines. Learning from the Suez campaign, the Memorandum accompanying the 1959-60 Air Estimates said that 'it is not only in the nuclear roles that the V-bombers are so valuable. If need be, they can be used, together with other aircraft of Bomber Command, to deliver a heavy weight of conventional bombs'.

On 29 October 1957, three No 214 Sqn Valiants left Marham for Changi on Exercise *Profiteer* – described as 'an operation designed to enable V-force crews to gain experience in operating in climatic conditions peculiar to the Far East'. However, there is no evidence that any V-bomber supported the ground fighting during the Malayan Emergency. Essentially, jet bombers were too sophisticated for Operation *Firedog* offensive air support operations, which were best left to the much more effective, piston-engined, Lincolns and Hornets. According to the No 214 Sqn ORB, the Far East excursion 'went without a hitch', with training flights from Changi including one to Vientiane, in Laos, by two Valiants – 'the first time jet aircraft had been seen in Laotian skies'.

No 90 Sqn sent two Valiants to Changi on 2 March 1958, a detachment authorised by Operation Order 1/58 (*Profiteer*) which said that 'two Valiant aircraft, three aircrews and ground servicing personnel will be detached from 4 March for approximately 14 days'. The purpose was to exercise crews in Far East operations, and the jets were to be 'fully equipped to operate in the conventional role' under the operational control of C-in-C Far East Air Force (FEAF), AM the Earl of Bandon.

Valiant sorties from Changi 'consisted mainly of simulated first-run attacks on certain specified airfields to collect target information for HQ FEAF'. Return flights were routed so as to 'give maximum practice to the radar defence and fighter interceptors in the Singapore area'. On two occasions 'aircraft flew through cumulo-nimbus cloud. During a first-run attack on an airfield in North Borneo, severe turbulence was encountered at 48,000 ft and the attack was abandoned. On return to base [it was discovered that] a considerable amount of resin paint had been stripped from the radome'.

No 148 Sqn detached four aircraft to RAAF Butterworth, Malaya, from 3 to 24 February 1959. 'The Valiants, supported by a Comet, went via El Adem, Nairobi, Karachi and Katunayake, in Ceylon. Flying

C-in-C FEAF, AM the Earl of Bandon, being saluted by Peter Clifton at Butterworth in June 1959. Crew chief Frank Roe is in the white overall. Accompanying the Earl is OC No 138 Sqn, Wg Cdr Sidney 'Tubby' Baker (*Don Briggs*)

commenced on 10 February, with familiarisation flights around Malaya. All crews then completed two long sorties over Borneo and Malaya, taking radar photographs of airfields and towns at the request of HQ FEAF'. Such detachments were designed to exercise air- and groundcrews in the rapid reinforcement of the FEAF, and to provide them with operating experience in the Far East theatre. However, when a Valiant showed the flag over Saigon or the Philippines, it was proving to both friends and allies that the UK was still capable of exerting influence around the world, while overawing potential opponents in the process.

Although Main Force Valiants went hither and yon, it was No 543 Sqn that really bestrode the globe. The battleship HMS *Valiant* took part in the Battle of Jutland, and the ship's motto was 'Valiant and Vigilant'. In February 1956 the CO of No 543 Sqn, 'Tich' Havercroft, was presented with a silver tankard used in *Valiant's* wardroom by Earl Mountbatten of Burma. The unit adopted the battleship's motto as well.

No 543 Sqn had begun life as the Main Force photographic reconnaissance (PR) squadron, and it operated independently as a lodger unit at RAF Gaydon from 24 September 1955. The squadron progressively moved to RAF Wyton, and its B Flight graduated from No 232 OCU a month later. However, by January 1956 there were still only enough Valiants for A Flight, the newcomers having to make do with a borrowed aircraft from Marham and sending one crew to Wittering to keep current on a No 138 Sqn B 1. Indeed, it was not until 9 February that No 543 Sqn was able to make a contribution to national defence when it took part in a Bomber Command V-force Interception Trial, providing two B 1s out of a force of seven Valiants and 18 Canberras to see how fighters and radar defences dealt with a mass penetration.

By April, when the squadron strength was up to eight Valiants, a sortie to Iceland and return was included in the cross-country exercises. During May No 543 Sqn took part in Bomber Command Exercise *Rejuvenate*, which was designed to give Fighter Command interception practice in the northwest approaches to the UK. The Swiss were impressed by a low-level No 543 Sqn Valiant flypast at the Zurich airshow in May 1956.

The following month the Havercroft crew took a Valiant to Idris to participate in Exercise *Thunderhead*, which put NATO defences in the northeastern Mediterranean to the test. At the same time, a No 543 Sqn

Valiant B(PR)K 1 WZ394 of No 543 Sqn is prepared for its next sortie at a sunny Wyton. In July 1964, whilst participating in Operation *Pontifex* over Southern Rhodesia, this aircraft became the first Valiant to suffer a rear spar crack

Valiant started flight trialling the H2S Mk 9 Yellow Aster Mk 1. Once the NBC and H2S radar were fitted, weather was no longer a barrier to reconnaissance. In general terms, the slower an H2S radar scanner turned, the sharper the picture and more detail that could be derived from it. If the scanner was stopped altogether, allowing the Valiant to do the moving, and a scan was produced every seven yards at right-angle-to-track on 35 mm film, the result approached that of a conventional photograph.

In November 1956 the No 543 Sqn ORB reported that flights had been 'severely restricted, due to the absence of several aircraft at Vickers-Armstrong Ltd, Weybridge, and Marshalls Ltd, Cambridge, for major modification and servicing', but 'now that fully modified aircraft are becoming available, seven-hour cross-countries have been initiated for general research into flight planning, fuel loading and jet performance'.

From 9 October to 29 December 1956, a pair of No 543 Sqn Valiants was detached to RCAF Namao on Operation *Snow Trip* – a joint Ministry of Supply/Bomber Command project to assess the effect on airborne radar equipment during late winter thaw and early spring conditions. Normally, water showed as black and land returns showed as 'bright ups' on the H2S. There was a reversal of returns over frozen or snowed-covered tundra. But it was not until May 1957 that No 543 Sqn was up and running with enough NBS-equipped Valiant B(PR) 1s to demonstrate its true potential. The ORB recorded that 'this month the squadron took part in its first operational reconnaissance during Exercise *Vigilant* – two crews flew each night carrying out radar targeting raids'.

Doug Skinner was a Nav Plotter in those early days, and he recalled that once Marshalls Ltd replaced the B(PR) 1 bomb-bay doors with their optical glass flats, through which each camera took its pictures, it would have been too big a task to convert them back to bombers The original doors were put in storage, but it is believed that rats ate the wiring!

In the beginning Doug recalled that No 543 Sqn's primary role was to provide damage assessment photography, with so many targets allocated to each crew. Photography 'obtained from various heights and with both radial and sidescan radar' over Canada during Phase III of Operation *Snow Trip* 'will undoubtedly advance the squadron's operational role'. Nevertheless, it soon became clear that venturing over the USSR after a nuclear exchange was nonsense, and in Doug Skinner's words, 'despite doing target study, it died very quickly'.

The 1950s saw a steady decline in the status of PR in the RAF compared to the heady wartime days of 1942, when a PR Spitfire or Mosquito could range at will over Hitler's Germany. Suez had proved to be a strategic reconnaissance debacle, with mountains of prints being brought back by PR Canberras, only to find that there was no mechanism in place to get the best out of them. To meet the reconnaissance needs of the jet age, the RAF decided once more to combine all its UK strategic reconnaissance assets into one Group. Thus, the Central Reconnaissance Establishment (CRE) came into being to control both the Joint Air Reconnaissance Intelligence Centre (JARIC) at Brampton and the UK Reconnaissance Force, comprising No 58 Sqn PR Canberras, No 543 Sqn SR Valiants and the Sigint Comets and Canberras of No 51 Sqn, all based at Wyton.

From 18 August 1956 onwards, No 543 Sqn had two B(PR) 1s (WZ391 and WZ392) on detachment to Edinburgh Field as part of Air Task Group Antler supporting the *Buffalo* nuclear tests at Maralinga Range. The unit's task was to carry out radar and photographic reconnaissance before, during and after each of the three nuclear explosions on 14 and 25 September and 9 October 1957. According to the detachment commander, Sqn Ldr Cremer, the PR Valiants and their crews did all that was expected of them, although several sorties had to be aborted due to weather conditions on the range;

'On the postponement of a shot firing, aircraft and crews reverted to standby. As the Valiants were based 450 miles away, it happened that they would be airborne before the cancellation was announced, which meant a loss of two-and-a-half hours' flying as the jet reduced its fuel load to a safe landing weight. On one occasion the cancellation was received when two B(PR) 1s were at the point of brakes off, with ten seconds to takeoff.'

From departure from Wyton on 18 August to return on 22 October, the detachment, in the words of Sqn Ldr Cremer, was 'most successful, both from the point of view of the transit flights and the operations

Wyton's finest – A No 543 Sqn Valiant B(PR) 1 in formation with a No 51 Sqn Canberra B 2 (left) and a No 58 Sqn Canberra PR 9 (right)

carried out at Edinburgh Field'. Another No 543 Sqn Valiant returned to Australia in July 1958 to photograph Blue Steel stand-off missile trials.

Although the performance of the Valiant B(PR) 1 was not much greater than that of the Canberra PR 7, it could fly 1500 miles further when fitted with drop tanks. PR Valiants were particularly useful because of the number of cameras they could carry. All were operated from one of two control panels, one on the starboard cabin wall and the other in the prone bombing station. The camera fit on trials Valiant WP205 in 1955 consisted of six F52 cameras with 36-in lenses arranged in a fan, plus a seventh as a port-facing oblique. In addition, it could carry a fan of three F49 survey cameras (two with 6-in lenses and one with 12-in) for wide-area coverage, one in the crate and two aft of the bomb-bay.

The six F52s would fire six times to give 36 pictures of the area covered by the 12-in vertical F49. The two 6-in F49s, one on either each side of the fuselage, together with the 12-in vertical F49, gave horizon-to-horizon coverage, and were christened the Trimet. Finally, there was one F49, with either a 6-in or 12-in lens, placed just aft of the camera crate on the fuselage floor.

The USAF believed that there was no substitute for focal length, and it went on to develop 100-in and 240-in lenses in preparation for the day when strategic reconnaissance aircraft would operate at 100,000 ft. But the greater the focal length, the smaller the area of coverage, and the British fought shy of sacrificing area coverage for scale. So, to obtain the best of both worlds, the RAF installed fans of cameras to provide horizon-to-horizon cover.

For night work, the PR Valiant crate carried five cameras in arrowhead formation to ensure that they looked ahead and to the sides of the exploding 250-lb photoflashes. These 25-million candlepower photoflashes were carried in a flash crate at the rear of the bomb-bay. The camera lens was open during the run-in, and as the photoflash was operated by a barostatic fuse, the film was exposed and the shutter closed. The film wound on before the shutter opened again, waiting for the next flash to go off. The night system was operated by the Nav Radar using the

Valiant B(PR)K 1s of No 543 Sqn bask in the Mediterranean sunshine on the pan at Luqa, Malta

'Bomb' function of the NBS. At least one No 543 Sqn crew deployed 'somewhere' operationally with five cameras and photoflashes.

A radar mosaic of the UK was completed in early 1958, and the first of several Sunspot detachments went to Malta to experience operating in sunny climes and to take part in the first night photo-flash drops over the Libyan desert. This was the only place available to practice dropping photo flares, which had to be done regularly so as to stay current. No 543 Sqn also had the dubious distinction of a court martial for the first Valiant taxiing accident, although the pilot, who had flown a Sunderland up the Yangtze during the *HMS Amethyst* incident in April 1949, was cleared of all blame.

A No 543 Sqn crew pose for the camera during a trip to Jamaica. They are, from left to right, Phil Farley (captain), Trev Phillips (co-pilot), Jimmy Brown (Nav Plotter), Alan Brooks (Nav Radar), Jock Hamilton (AEO) and Unknown (Crew Chief). The crane squadron crest is visible on the drop tank behind the crew (*Alan Brooks*)

The standard Valiant aircrew tour length back then was six years. Nav Radar Alan Brooks was posted in to replace the solitary SNCO Nav Radar, Flt Sgt Len Terry, in 1959. There was always a crew on two hours standby for a week at a time, this arrangement pre-dating the formal Quick Reaction Alert (QRA) used by the Main Force – a reconnaissance crew just got airborne as quickly as possible, and because each situation was unique, there was no opportunity for detailed pre-flight planning.

Alan recalled his crew being called out during the gales and snowstorms that blitzed Sheffield over 16/17 February 1962. Wind speeds reaching 96 mph damaged two-thirds of the houses in the city, and three people were killed. 'It was like flying into a white envelope – snow on the ground and lowering snow cloud above – so we relied on the H2S radar to keep clear of the Pennines. The vertical photographs taken down through the snowfall were surprisingly good, and depicted whole rows of roofless houses.

'We would go out into the Atlantic to 30 degrees W, turn North, then come running in flat out to test the UK air defences. On one of these occasions we got a message that two ships had collided off Iceland. We went to look and found lots of black smoke – you couldn't see through it, but Yellow Aster put a new volcano called Surtsey on the map. It was hard to plan for eventualities like this before takeoff.'

Given all this activity, it was not surprising that someone on No 543 Sqn put pen to paper about the Valiant's potential for maritime radar reconnaissance (MRR). Tony Banfield joined the RAF aged 17 on a Direct Entry commission. He went to the Gaydon OCU in March 1958, before joining No 49 Sqn as a co-pilot. At the age of 24 he moved to No 543 Sqn as a captain in August 1962, just as the bulk of the squadron detached out to Tehran. 'We were very much a recce outfit', said Tony. 'There was nothing Main Force about it. CRE did its own thing. The squadron had a number of standard UK tasks, as weather and crew availability permitted'.

The Banfield crew was involved early on with Operation *Agat*. These were ten-hour sorties, with the Valiant cruise-climbing north on the lookout for Soviet ships. The nav team had to learn quickly about the intricacies of high latitude navigation as they ventured into the Spitzbergen area and around the North Cape at the edge of the ice pack.

The NBS on No 543 Sqn Valiants had modifications that were not on Main Force equipment, the most important from an MRR perspective being the three million scale. The Valiant's H2S radar could look out to a range of approximately 180 nautical miles when at 40,000 ft altitude, but this whole radar picture would have required a 27-in radar display. Unfortunately, the Nav Radar only had a 9-in circular radar display. Various scales could be displayed on the screen, and by moving the timebase origin away from the screen centre with a small joy stick – known as the '626' – the Nav Radar could see out to 180 nautical miles. However, the three million scale selection allowed the No 543 Sqn Nav Radar to see the whole picture radar at once. This was of no use for detailed ship recognition, but as H2S Mk 9 transmissions could be picked up by the average interception receiver some 500 miles ahead of the Valiant, the three million scale was very useful up in the far north, where it paid to keep out of trouble.

On the Banfield crew, Nav Radar Arthur Creighton took 15-minute sun shots while the AEO monitored the Norwegian air defence radar system for warnings of any Soviet fighters scrambling from Archangel or Murmansk. The Banfield crew, who became *Agat* specialists, flew a castellated series of rectangles from east to west. They were not searching for any specific threat (as far as they knew), and the early *Agat* flights were very much trials employing the camera crate as well as the radar – 'if you got good stuff on film, that was a bonus'. They once found a Soviet naval vessel doing a rate of knots, so Tony Banfield pulled into a 40-degree bank turn and took a photo using a long focal length F96 camera. He got a great shot of the ship for which the Royal Navy was to be very grateful 'but it was purely by chance'. After many hours of cruise-climbing, the Valiant would transit back to base at around 52,000 ft.

Agat had its moments. 'In June 1963, the nav team mistook Iceland for the Shetlands on the H2S and by the time they corrected their error, we only just managed to scrape back into RNAS Lossiemouth. The Royal Navy was not pleased to be directed to put a double guard on the aircraft overnight before we returned to Wyton'.

An awful lot of MRR was done in August 1963, although it was written up in the logbooks as 'shippex'. 'We never knew what the other crews were doing', said Alan Brooks. 'Everyone kept that very close to their chests. On one occasion, two Valiants left Bahrain on a single flight plan and we didn't see the other one until we both landed at Aden!'

The most visible No 543 Sqn tasks tended to be survey work such as the 1961 detachment to help the local authorities in British Honduras assess damage caused by Hurricane Hattie. The exposed film had to be flown back home for processing via British Airways. Other relief work included damage assessment photography over the severely devastated Moroccan port of Agadir, which had been struck by an earthquake in February 1960. Around 15,000 people (about a third of the city's population) were killed, another 12,000 injured and at least

35,000 people left homeless. It was said that No 543 Sqn crews were sent to photograph the damage because it was the nearest a city would look after a nuclear attack.

In 1959 three detachments went to survey Thailand under Operation *Segment*, and also to photograph the Kariba Dam in Zambia. The Thailand missions were flown from RAAF Butterworth, and some 76,095 square miles were duly photographed, together with 1000 square miles of Borneo. No 543 Sqn returned to Butterworth in 1961 to complete the Thai survey – crews

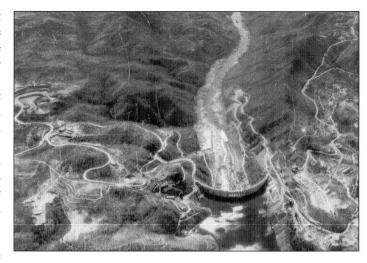

did three-month detachments overflying the country outside the rainy season when the sky was crystal clear.

A crew would takeoff from Butterworth with two sets of film magazines, expose one, land at Bangkok to change magazines, fly a second day and then land back at Butterworth for processing. 'While at Butterworth for the Thai survey', recalled Alan Brooks, 'we flew some sorties over Malaya and the Kra Isthmus in support of ground troops. I personally took some reasonably low pictures in the Alor Star area. Although the Emergency had been declared over, it was re-introduced while we were there, and all of the detachment were issued with the General Service Medal (Malaya)'.

In early 1960, a single Valiant surveyed the Seychelles – Exercise *Obliquity* – before transiting home through Embakasi airfield, Nairobi. From there, three sorties were flown to photograph all around the borders

A No 543 Sqn photograph of the Kariba Dam in Zambia, this shot being taken in 1959 (*Alan Brooks*)

The No 543 Sqn detachment at RAAF Butterworth, Malaya, in early 1961. The Valiant bears the flag of OC No 543 Sqn, Wg Cdr C J StD Jefferies (seen here sitting *without* his legs crossed in the front row), a former Battle of Malta Hurricane ace (*Alan Brooks*)

of what is now Somalia, leaving PR Canberra crews to fill the gaps in between. A photo and radar survey of the Marion, Gough and Tristan group of islands was made in 1961. This No 543 Sqn detachment was based at Ysterplaat, in South Africa, but the sorties had to be flown from D F Malan airport because its 6900 ft runway was the only one in the Cape capable of accommodating the Valiant. In June 1962 a detachment flew to Townsville, in Queensland, from where it started surveying the Solomon and Santa Cruz Islands, plus 53 per cent of the New Hebrides. In all, 6643 miles of photographs were taken in 47 sorties, some of which were flown from Port Moresby, in New Guinea, and some from Nandi, in Fiji. This was completed in June 1963.

In 1964 No 543 Sqn was involved in the largest PR task ever undertaken by the RAF. Known as Operation *Pontifex*, this involved the survey of the greater part of the Rhodesias and Bechuanaland. Three Valiants, four crews and 100 support personnel were based at New Sarum, near Salisbury, and over 11 weeks from June a total of 110 sorties were flown and more than 27,000 photographs taken, processed and printed, plotted and assessed. The detachment flew 66,154 miles of flight lines, covering an area of more than 400,000 square miles – greater than the UK, France and Germany. Errors of up to 16 miles were discovered on previous maps, and features like Lake Bangweula were found to be a different shape from those on existing charts.

No official records seeking or giving ministerial approval for peripheral operations by No 543 Sqn Valiants have come to light, although on one occasion the Station Commander at RAF Wyton was heard to remark, 'I must be the only Station Commander with three squadrons, all of whom make sorties authorised at Cabinet level'. On the MRR side,

No 543 Sqn mapping the bridge over the River Kwai in 1961. The memorial to those who died building the railway is in the southeast corner at the end of the track (*Alan Brooks*)

one aircrew member recalled flying from Lossiemouth up over the Kola Peninsula looking for Soviet submarines venturing out once the ice had melted, but there was nothing resembling U-2 type operations. And following the downing of a USAF RB-47H while probing in the Kola area, a restriction was placed on No 543 Sqn operating beyond 24 degrees East, not that there is evidence of any crew having ever flown that far.

The nearest the unit came to flying a 'hush-hush' mission was when a PR Valiant was routed to run along the northern Turkish border. The crew was given the codeword for the Nike missile batteries in case of any Soviet response. Was the Valiant sent that way so that a No 51 Sqn 'ferret' could listen for any reaction? No 543 Sqn crew members never knew.

READY FOR ARMAGEDDON

A Valiant dispersal could be a cold and frosty place in winter

Four types of Valiant entered service. The Type 706 was the B 1, the Type 710 was the B(PR) 1 (ten built), the Type 733 was the B(PR)K 1 (14 built), which met a requirement that some tankers should have a PR capability, and the Type 758 was the B(K) 1 bomber/tanker (44 built).

The Valiant force took a number of years to attain full operational capability, not least because the UK had taken on the Herculean task of rebuilding the homeland after 1945 while creating a nuclear capability plus *three* separate V-bombers from scratch. Some Valiant Main Force units had to wait years for NBS components through delays in production and service clearance of airborne equipment. RCM/ECM was not available in effective strength until 1959. AEO Brian Matthews was on a No 49 Sqn Main Force crew with a dedicated war target, but there were no ECM warning devices fitted to the unit's Valiants before he left in 1960.

On 16 July 1958, Prime Minister Harold Macmillan reaffirmed the purpose of the British independent nuclear capability as follows;

'(a) To retain our special relation with the USA and, through it, our influence in world affairs, and, especially, our right to have a voice in the final issue of peace or war.

'(b) To make a definite, though limited, contribution to the total nuclear strength of the West, while recognising that the USA must play the major part in maintaining the balance of nuclear power.

'(c) To enable us, by threatening to use our independent nuclear power, to secure US cooperation in a situation in which their interests were less immediately threatened than our own.

'(d) To make sure that, in a nuclear war, sufficient attention is given to certain Soviet targets that are of greater importance to us than to the USA [particularly bomber airfields and missile-launching sites from which attacks on the UK could be mounted].

'To constitute a minimum deterrent and serve the purposes for which it is intended, the V-force must be operationally viable – i.e. it must be sufficiently large and well equipped to deliver enough bombs to inflict an adequate measure of destruction in Russia.'

Talks in early 1957 between the RAF CAS and his USAF opposite number had resulted in the targeting plans of SAC and Bomber Command being closely dovetailed. By December 1958, SAC had 380 B-52s and 1367 B-47s in its bomber force, compared with the RAF's 45 Valiants, 18 Vulcans and ten Victors. Despite the numerical differences, Bomber Command had the advantage of knowing that

Sqn Ldr Norfolk and his No 90 Sqn crew dropping a dummy Blue Danube atomic bomb from WP223 over the Jurby Range, off the Isle of Man, in May 1959

its progress in a war would be facilitated by US missiles, but it was not just a one-sided arrangement. 'Some of our targets', recalled one AEO, 'looked as if they were clearing the way for someone else', and in the words of former Deputy CAS, AM Sir Geoffrey Tuttle, 'we taught SAC a hell of a lot. We had to face many of the problems first – we were nearer to the USSR, we were threatened long before the Americans were, and therefore we had the incentive to survive much sooner than they did'.

Throughout the Cold War, the key target for the British GCHQ would remain the Soviet nuclear weapons programme, including ballistic missiles, bombers and other means of delivery. Under the Single Integrated Operational Plan (SIOP), total US/RAF strategic air forces were deemed sufficient to cover all Soviet targets, including airfields and air defence. Bomber Command's contribution had increased to 108 aircraft by June 1959, and they were allocated 106 targets – 69 cities, which were centres of government or of other military significance; 17 long-range air force airfields that constituted part of the Soviet nuclear threat; and 20 elements of the Soviet *PVO-Strany* air defence system

Valiant bomber squadrons became operational around the time that low-trajectory nuclear-tipped medium range missiles appeared in Soviet satellite territories. These threatened to wreak havoc on the UK within minutes of being launched, so the 1958 Defence White Paper revealed that measures were being taken to raise the V-force's 'state of readiness, so as to reduce to a minimum the time needed for takeoff'.

Leslie Worsdell, Marshalls' Chief Test Pilot, recalled proposals for a Valiant Rapid Take-Off Procedure;

'AOC No 3 Group didn't want his Valiants caught on the ground, so he asked Marshalls to find some means of getting the aircraft into the air with just five minutes warning time. The Valiant pre-flight procedure normally took 20, 25 or 30 minutes by the time all the covers had been taken off and the crew had gone through all the pre-flight drills. Our engineers came up with ingenious devices. There were two pitot tubes on the jet for the pick-up of pressure for the airspeed indicators. These were about four feet long and fixed on each wing tip, projecting forwards, but out of reach of anyone on the ground. To fit covers to keep out the weather and insects, and to remove them and their attendant warning flags before flight, the groundcrew had to get step-ladders. There was also an out of the way cover for the Q-Feel [a device that made the controls go heavier as the jet flew faster to avoid it being over-stressed] air intake that faced forward at the base of the fin on top of the fuselage.

'The solution for the pitot head covers and the Q-Feel cover was to spring-load them and attach them by tapes to fittings on the ground so that as the aircraft started to move, the triggers were pulled, the springs released, the covers shot forward out of the way and the jet was "clean".

'Normally, the engines had to be started one by one, as they initially put a very heavy discharge on the ground power units until they sped up and their own generators came on line. All this took time, so Marshalls' solution was to move the ground power unit connection beneath the fuselage, facing backwards, with heavy-duty starter ground power units connected to it behind the aircraft. With a suitable system of elastics and levers, as the aircraft moved forward the electrical and ground-to-aircraft intercom connections would disconnect by pull, the covering flap would spring closed and the electrical system was properly sealed off.

'To give more power for starting four engines at once, the ground power units were doubled or trebled in capacity. We had several practices at this. My co-pilot and I would sit in the aircraft all strapped in, and we had done "vital actions" as far as we could. The only thing we had to do was to press four starter buttons together to fire up the engines, taxi onto the runway, open the throttles and take off.

'One day the AOC said that he wanted to see what he was paying for. He came to me for a briefing, and almost immediately upon reaching the aircraft he said "Five-minute warning – GO!" With that we opened the throttles – opening the throttles during start-up to speed up the engines more quickly was quite against regulations – and pressed the four starter buttons at the same time. I throttled back, let the brakes off, started taxiing, turned onto the 200-yard loop and then onto the runway, which at that time was quite short, and took off. At 500 ft we raised the undercarriage, turned downwind, lowered the undercarriage, put down some more flap, turned in and landed before the five minutes were up.

'We thought we'd get medals for that, so we taxied in grinning, only to be met by an irate air vice-marshal, who said "I've never seen anything so bloody dangerous in all my life. How did you know those covers were going to come off?" I replied, "Well, somebody would have said stop if they hadn't". "You can't rely on that!", and I said, "Well, we could see". He said, "You couldn't see the Q-Feel one because that's still in the fin!" "No, you're quite right, sir", I agreed.

As advanced Vulcans and Victors arrived in service, Valiant bombers were assigned to the SACEUR as a Tactical Bomber Force. Several were placed at 15-minute readiness in case of surprise Soviet attack, and this QRA concept was progressively extended to the whole MBF. On 10 January 1963 C-in-C Bomber Command told CAS that from 1 April, 'I propose increasing the QRA force to 17 Vulcans and Victors (plus the four Valiants of the SACEUR Force), rising to 20 Victors and Vulcans by 1 July'. From now on, 20 per cent of the V-force would be nuclear armed and at permanent readiness 24 hours a day, 365 days a year.

The tactics to be employed by the V-force against targets in the Soviet Union were dictated by the performance of the aircraft. The maximum takeoff weight of a Valiant with drop tanks was 175,000 lbs, while that of the Victor B 2 was 223,000 lbs and the Vulcan B 2 204,000 lbs. Much of the difference was made up of fuel, which impacted on the Valiant's radius of action. On reaching top-of-climb, the Valiant pilot set the autopilot to fly the most economical cruise speed of Mach 0.75. As fuel was burnt off and all-up-weight reduced, the jet would gently 'cruise-climb' up towards its service ceiling of 54,000 ft. However, the relative lack of ECM protection constrained where the Valiants could go.

Derek Aldred was a 23-year-old ex-Canberra Nav Plotter when he joined No 7 Sqn at Honington in 1956. 'The Valiant was a gentleman's Canberra', he recalled, 'with four times the room down the back'. To Derek, dispersals seemed 'a bit of a game. Bells would ring, we'd fire up the engines and then go back in for breakfast. I even had a chart on which I had to draw Soviet SAM sites'.

The great advantage of the manned bomber over the missile is that the former could be launched to make a potential aggressor withdraw from the brink, whereas there is no way of bringing back a missile. V-bombers would have met timing points and specific positions in order to comply with the coordinated raid plan. The routes were planned to fly out to a 100-mile arc based on Flamborough Head, then tracks would fly to a straight line position known as the Go/No Go Line. No Valiants were allowed to cross this Line without the crew receiving a valid coded message. If no message came, there was no assuming that Whitehall had been obliterated – the V-force had to turn back. On the other hand, once the Go message had been received there was no recall mechanism.

To give some idea of a wartime mission, it is worth following the flight profile of the 1962 Bombing and Navigation Competition. After a scramble from home base, crews flew a high-altitude navex that included an astro-navigation leg to a point off the Netherlands, then northeastwards to a point off the Danish coast, northwards over Norway then southwestwards to Glasgow and Northern Ireland. From here it was eastwards back to Scotland and Newcastle, where the first of three simulated blind-bombing attacks were carried out against the southwest corner of a hangar on Ouston airfield, in Northumberland. The next two targets were the centre of the footbridge at Hooton railway station in Cheshire and the centre of the road junction in Enford village on Salisbury Plain. During these attacks crews encountered NBS jamming and used ECM against ground radar and made an evasive bombing run.

The April 1963 event was renamed the Bomber Command Combat Proficiency Competition, and it was described by the C-in-C as an 'annual stocktaking of our Operational State – an opportunity for crews and units to show what they are worth in the most stringent conditions, short of actual operations'. The new title had been introduced to emphasise that there were 'factors other than bombing and navigation equally vital to the success of an operational sortie in war'. A communications test en route required AEOs to record a message consisting of 50 four-letter groups transmitted from the Bomber Command W/T Control Centre at a speed of 22 words per minute. The competition had a preliminary

Aircrew to the left, groundcrew to the right – the race is on to meet the raised Alert state. They are running towards Valiant WZ396 of No 543 Sqn at Wyton

phase, flown during the first three months of the year, when 17 competing units (including Nos 49, 139, 148 and 207 Valiant Sqns) had to complete 12 sorties to decide which was to be awarded the Medium Bomber Squadron Efficiency Trophy.

How would the Valiants have coped against serious opposition? Notwithstanding the prophets of doom, the SAM did not make the bomber obsolete overnight. A Joint Intelligence Committee report forecast that Soviet city defences would be complete by 1961. Based on this assessment, Bomber Command aimed to reduce SAM effectiveness by ECM, tactical routeing to avoid known SAM sites and increasing the number of V-bombers allocated to important, heavily defended, targets.

The principal ground radar in the Russian Control and Reporting system was the 'Token' centimetric (S band) equipment. It was a multi-beam, continuous height-finding radar operating on five or seven frequencies. It was backed up by a chain of metric stations, most of which were of the 'Knife Rest' type operating on 65 to 75 mc/s, with the additional ability to operate on frequencies up to about 104 mc/s as an anti-jamming measure. These radars were very vulnerable to jamming. Moreover, Soviet ADF control operated in the conventional VHF band between 100 and 156 mc/s. This simple aircraft equipment was fairly vulnerable to ECM, despite the possibility of using a substantial high-power transmitter on the ground as an anti-countermeasure step.

Bill Massey flew with No 49 Sqn, and at high level 'the range of the Valiant wasn't too bad, provided you cruise-climbed. During *Grapple* support missions, we would fly for almost eight hours across the US without refuelling'. V-bombers would have entered the Soviet Union in cells of six, and the less endowed Valiants would have hoped to take advantage of the chaos as the Soviet air defence system went down.

Under certain circumstances, the Fishpool mode on the H2S radar could detect fighters around and below, so the Nav Radar could sometimes see the jets climbing. The Valiants' Orange Putter tail warning radar was designed to give captain and AEO visual indication, and all the crew aural warning, of a fighter coming within 170 degrees in azimuth and 80 degrees in elevation. The maximum range attainable was 4000 yards, with a 50 per cent probability of detection out to 3000 yards, which provided a reasonable degree of situational awareness.

As Derek Aldred recalled, 'the AEO had a simple dial which told him if anyone had got a lock-on'. Then it was down to bundles of Window tinfoil strips, which produced echoes equal in magnitude to those of a Valiant, to try to confuse a pilot relying on his airborne radar. While the Soviets could point their fighters straight at the bomber if they got good radar control from the ground to put them there, if they had not got it the interception of a Valiant at 50,000 ft became a lottery.

Having worked his way into the USSR, the Nav Radar could often

A No 7 Sqn crew probably at Offutt AFB, Nebraska, in July 1962. Standing in the foreground, from left to right, are Colin Mathieson (co-pilot), 'Mac' McCormick (AEO), Bob Wolstenholme (nav plotter), and Tony Cottingham (captain). The missing crew member is the nav radar, Wg Cdr Jack Wilson, OC No 7 Sqn (*Tony Cottingham*)

see his aim point from 160 miles away, and the usual procedure was to home to an easily identifiable Initial Point some 60 miles from weapon release, where the navigation and bombing computers could be finally updated accurately. At 40 miles to weapon release, the Nav Radar would change over to his larger bombing scale, placing the target under his aiming markers by means of his 'joystick'. If the target response was weak or impossible to identify, the bombing run could still be pressed home, provided there was an identifiable reference point nearby. The coordinate distances of the target from the reference point could be set on 'offset' dials, and the jet automatically homed to the correct release point.

Once the target or 'offsets' were in, the computers did the rest down to feeding steering information directly into the autopilot. The NBS was a marvellous piece of equipment that even opened the bomb-bay doors automatically just before the point where it computed that the bomb should be dropped. The weapon could be released automatically or manually, and as it left the bomb-bay, the pilot would rack his jet round into the escape manoeuvre to avoid overflying the detonation, close the bomb-bay doors and beat a retreat. If the crew could not make it to a friendly airfield, the Valiant was equipped with two destructors stowed on the outside of the pressure cabin fairing and aft of the sextant dome.

Exercise *Green Epoch* was held between 13-17 February 1957 to give the air defences of the US Navy's Sixth Fleet the opportunity to deal with attacking bombers. During the first two days No 148 Sqn Valiants carried out eight night attacks, followed by four day attacks on 16 February. Only one interception was made by a pair of carrier-based Grumman F9F-9 Cougars in afterburner at 40,000 ft – the remaining Cougars were seen trying vainly to get to height. The attack plan was quite simple. An initial diversionary feint had drawn the defenders into the air, whereupon the Valiant intruders turned and flew back out of range. They returned 35 minutes later, just as the defending fighters were running out of fuel. The fleet was attacked successfully and none of the Valiants were claimed as shot down.

In April 1959, two Vulcans and four Valiants from Marham deployed to Goose Bay, Labrador, for Exercise *Eyewasher*. The V-bombers flew on the night of 25/26 April 1959 'to exercise the Eastern Air Defence Command of North America'. Their objective was to penetrate the DEW (Distant Early Warning) Line in northeast Canada, and the subsequent report stated that the Valiants of No 148 Sqn were over Frobisher at 42,000 ft and the Vulcans at 48,000 ft. Only one of the six aircraft was formally challenged.

UK signal intelligence at the time showed that Moscow's command and control system was poor, radar coverage was patchy and fighter reaction times were slow. Former fighter ace turned V-bomber commander 'Johnnie' Johnson thought that his aircraft would have been very vulnerable if they had gone in during daylight independently from the USAF. But Johnson, whose firsthand experience of bomber and fighter operations was second to none, believed that as many as 85-90 per cent of the V-force would have got through at night as part of a coordinated US-UK operation. His boss at HQ Bomber Command, Sir Harry Broadhurst, was equally convinced that his force was good enough to deter a potential enemy from committing the supreme act of folly.

ON THE WAY DOWN

By the end of 1959, the RAF had a national stockpile of only 71 fission bombs. The Yellow Sun family of thermonuclear fusion weapons was only arriving in dribs and dabs, and it was not surprising that the original requirement for carriage of a megaton bomb in the Valiants was cancelled, in part to save costs. To bridge the shortfall, an agreement had been reached with Washington whereby 168 US-built nuclear weapons would be made available for use on V-bombers and Canberras in time of war.

By 1959 some 72 RAF medium bombers were armed with what were known as Project 'E' weapons. Blue Danube was replaced by the Red Beard tactical atomic bomb designed around an all-plutonium 15 KT warhead. With an improved implosion concept (air lenses), Red Beard weighed only 2000 lbs, but by 1962 there were only enough of them to match eight Valiants – the remainder of the Valiant force relied on the Mk 5 6000-lb atomic bomb obtained under Project 'E'. It was a war-fighting weapon as distinct from the thermonuclear Yellow Sun 2 free-fall bomb and Blue Steel missile warhead which, when aimed at targets like downtown Moscow, were deterrent in nature.

Back in late 1957 the Air Council had considered how to 'make the best use of Valiants that would become surplus to the frontline in 1961' as Mk 2 Vulcans and Victors came on line. The obvious option was to use some Valiants as tactical bombers to replace SACEUR-assigned Bomber Command Canberras that lacked an autonomous, all-weather blind-bombing capability. However, as Valiants would be more expensive to run, it was suggested that 64 Canberras should be replaced by just 24 Valiants. SACEUR gave his approval on the assumption that one Valiant would replace two nuclear-capable Canberras.

There were three possible weapons if the Valiant was to be given a dual carriage capability – the Mk 5, which currently armed most Valiants under Project 'E', the Mk 7 (1650-lb) currently carried by the Canberras and the Mk 28 lightweight weapon, not then supplied under Project 'E'. The Mk 28 was deemed 'the most suitable weapon to provide a dual carriage capability', and a modification programme, including clearance trials, to enable three squadrons of Valiants to carry it would take about 12 months to complete at a cost of between £150,000 and £250,000.

Once the US government agreed that the Mk 28 bomb could be supplied under Project 'E', feasibility studies indicated that it would be technically possible to achieve an Initial Operating Capability by April 1961, building up to a Tactical Bomber Force (TBF) of 24 Valiant aircraft by June. With effect from 1 January 1960, No 207 Sqn was operationally at the disposal of SACEUR, but C-in-C Bomber Command was responsible directly to him for operational readiness

SACEUR Gen Lauris Norstad (standing at right) at Marham on 13 October 1960 inspecting the Valiants that will become his all-weather Tactical Bomber Force. SACEUR is accompanied by C-in-C Bomber Command, Sir Kenneth Cross

A No 207 Sqn crew at a NATO Defence College display at RAF Wittering. They are, from left to right, Mike Harrington (captain), John Potter (co-pilot), Harry Brunt (nav plotter), Denis Mooney (nav radar), Alan Webb (AEO) and Chief Tech Millar (Crew Chief) (*No 207 Sqn Association*)

and efficiency of the force. Bomber Command Operational Centre (BCOC) was linked by direct telephone lines with SHAPE (Supreme Headquarters Allied Powers Europe) Operational Centre. SACEUR's orders were passed directly to BCOC by this line and from there to Marham on the Bomber Command network.

On 1 and 13 July 1961, respectively, Nos 49 and 148 Sqns joined No 207 Sqn on assignment to SACEUR in the tactical bomber role, No 49 Sqn having moved across from Wittering to Marham in June 1961. 'The squadron is now committed to keep one aircraft and one crew at 15 minutes' readiness in the QRA dispersal', wrote the No 49 Sqn ORB. The 24 TBF Valiants were cleared for dual carriage of Mk 28 weapons from 13 July 1961.

Mike Harrington joined No 207 Sqn as a captain at Marham. 'The US weapons were very sexy things – white and shiny and looking very mean'. Armourer Pete Sharp found that the Project 'E' bombs 'were much easier to load all round. There was no fiddling with electric heating blankets, and only one set of connectors to deal with, whereas Blue Danube and Red Beard required lots of bomb-bay furnishings, snatch latches, cable retraction drums and fin extension lanyard packs. They were always a pain to mess with. I used to feel that the RAF took better care of its weapons than its personnel as far as warmth went'.

Wg Cdr R D Alexander, whose crew was Select Star on No 148 Sqn, went on a course with his Nav Radar, Flt Lt K Alport, at RAE Farnborough on the Mk 28 weapon, which had a warhead variable in destructive power from 60 to 100 KT. The pair of them went because a 'two-man principle' applied to all nuclear arming and release procedures. To make it impossible for any single individual to sabotage or fire a nuclear weapon, it took two men to arm the bomb before takeoff, and the codeword for weapon release was split such that the captain and Nav Radar had half the valid alphanumeric each.

Each Valiant crew had two SACEUR targets – a primary and a secondary (another crew's in case they fell down), plus a National target. None of the crews knew each other's targets, and when they went off on an exercise sortie ('Edom', which tested the crews' reaction times, 'Mick' or 'Checkmate'), they carried 'Go' bags containing their

flight plans, which were updated according to the latest Intelligence information. Another exercise was 'Titton', its object, explained in the No 49 Sqn ORB for September 1961, being 'to give crews a more realistic experience of what a possible operational sortie would contain'.

SACEUR-assigned Valiants did not deploy to a diversion airfield because the Americans had to 'retain custody at Marham of all special weapons on QRA and provide a minimum of one US custodial with each weapon on alert status'.

In September 1960, No 207 Sqn was involved in NATO exercises *Flashback* and *Swordthrust II*. '*Flashback* commenced at 1200 hrs on 20 September, when the six crews participating were brought to 45-minute readiness. "Scramble" was given by SACEUR, through HQ Bomber Command, at 0715 hrs on 21 September. *Flashback* involved the simulated attack on targets in southern Europe and *Swordthrust II* the search for, and simulated attacks on, the aircraft carriers of Carrier Strike Group Two in the Lofoten Islands sea area, and simulated attacks on selected Norwegian and UK targets'.

'Spike' Milligan was a Nav Plotter on No 49 Sqn. 'There was no standby commitment at Wittering, but we were on QRA at Marham for 48 hours at a stretch, in flying suits behind the barbed wire at 15-minute readiness at all times'. The QRA crew was housed during the day in a suitably equipped rest room in the Operations block, and at night in a five-berth caravan – meals were provided in the aircrew buffet. The money for all this was provided by SACEUR, but the downside was the presence of a US armed guard, even into the cockpit at times.

Dual carriage high-level Mk 28 bombs were dropped from 45,000 ft, but 'Spike' Milligan recalled that 'we started to go low-level almost immediately'. In a letter dated 26 January 1962, C-in-C Bomber Command stated that the build-up of Soviet defensive systems had greatly reduced the Valiants' chances of survival at high level. Having no ECM and being too slow to be routed in company with ECM-equipped Vulcans and Victors, they were vulnerable not only to missile defences and the latest Soviet fighters, but also to older MiG-17 'Fresco' jets, which still formed the bulk of the Soviet fighter force. There was now no area within

No 214 Sqn Valiant WZ390 is towed past Bloodhound SAMs at Marham in 1963. Each V-force bomber base had dedicated missile batteries to protect it. The detachable pylons that carried the Valiant's underwing tanks were also designed to carry 30 ft-long nacelles to increase the aircraft's conventional bomb load by up to 12 1000-lb bombs per wing, but this requirement was cancelled in August 1956

range of Bomber Command aircraft that was not defended by supersonic fighters, and no worthwhile target not defended by SAMs.

The answer was to descend to low-level at the edge of Soviet early warning radar cover and to run in to the target flying nap of the earth. The changeover to low-level, parachute-retarded lay-down Mk 43 weapons occurred during 1963. TBF Valiants were to carry two Mk 43s as with the Mk 28, and in its ORB for April 1963, No 207 Sqn recorded that 'on the very first day of the month the squadron, with the other SACEUR units at Marham, received the Mk 43 weapon from the USAF, and so operationally has a true low-level capability, being able to attack targets at low-level. For National targets, however, we are still committed to the "pop-up" attack'.

Vickers had given much thought to low-level operations, and its Type 673 Pathfinder was the most impressive Valiant derivative. Conceived in 1948, it came from an Air Staff request to English Electric and Vickers to convert certain Canberras and Valiants to act as special Pathfinders, equipped with extra avionics and strengthened to go in over targets at high-speed and low-level, dropping target markers for the main force. Each firm came up with a 'one-off' prototype – the Canberra B 5 and the Valiant B 2 – but only Vickers had to undertake a major structural re-design to meet the requirement.

The Pathfinder Valiant's sea-level speed was to be around 552 mph instead of the airframe-limited 414 mph of the B 1, so the main stress-bearing structure had to be strengthened. As the whole outer wing torsion box had to be kept intact, this strengthening was effected by filling in the big hole in the outer wing that accommodated the undercarriage – the main wheel bogies were modified to retract backwards into nacelles projecting behind the leading edge. Apart from lengthening the fuselage by 4 ft 6 in and generally reinforcing the rest of the structure, the only other difference lay in the addition of extra fuel tankage in the space where the old undercarriage had been because Vickers was not sure what low-level range would be asked of its Pathfinder.

The Pathfinder, or Valiant B 2 as it was christened, was the last prototype to be built at the Fox Warren experimental shop, and it was first flown by Jock Bryce, with Brian Trubshaw as co-pilot, on 11 April 1952. Painted in a glossy black night finish overall, the Pathfinder Valiant looked a terrifying sight as it hurtled along at low level. It was powered by Avon RA 14 engines, and the prototype was supposed to lead to an even more impressive machine propelled by Rolls-Royce Conways,

The Pathfinder Valiant B 2 prototype WJ954 was painted black overall for night operations. Seventeen production models were ordered (WZ389 to WZ405), but they were eventually cancelled, and additional B 1s were produced instead

but by then the RAF had decided that perhaps Pathfinders were irrelevant in the NBS age and the Valiant B 2 was abandoned.

Navigation and bombing equipment in the Valiant B 1 was not unduly degraded by low-level flight down to 250 ft above ground level. In fact the low-level attack phase improved NBS weapon-aiming accuracy to 250 yards, and further refinement was possible because pilots could now map read and pass accurate fixes back to the nav team.

It was envisaged from the start that low-level flying training would be conducted over the UK, North America and possibly North Africa, and the hazards peculiar to low-level flying – turbulence, impact damage (from hailstones and bird strikes), visibility and temperature – were spelt out. Weapons to be used on the Valiant in the low-level role were outlined in May 1964 as the 'Mk 43 lay-down bomb, and possibly Red Beard in pop-up delivery'. For camouflage, the metal uppersurfaces of Valiants were to be 'coloured by a variegated pattern of greys and greens', while undersurfaces could remain in the white anti-flash finish.

'Spike' Milligan recalled that crews retained their high-level expertise for the transit legs, but there was now much more emphasis placed on operating down low. 'There was no problem in operating at low-level – the Valiant was a good, stable platform'. According to another Nav Plotter, 'we had the range to just about make the furthest part of East Germany'. Mike Harrington would go on to fly Vulcan B 2s, and he recalled that piloting the Valiant at low-level 'was exactly the same as on the Vulcan, apart from the lack of Terrain Following Radar. The Nav Radar could see the cut off on hills up ahead from his screen, and he would give a running commentary. This eventually got stamped on for being unsafe. We didn't think about airframe fatigue in those days'.

When the Valiant TBF was established at Marham in 1961 there were still three other Valiant squadrons in the Main Force. At the beginning of 1962, C-in-C Bomber Command asked the Air Ministry to approve the modification of these aircraft for low-level operations. In the event, the Valiant contribution to the MBF came to an end during 1962. No 90 Sqn at Honington was

A Vulcan B 2, Valiant B 1 and Victor B 2 in low-level camouflage sit side-by-side at Goose Bay, Labrador, in 1964

Newly camouflaged Valiants of No 49 Sqn on the ORP at Marham in 1964. XD829, in the foreground, served with No 49 Sqn throughout its service career, participating in the *Grapple* trials soon after being delivered to the unit in 1956

This Marham-based Valiant B(K) 1 bears a No 49 Sqn crest beneath its cockpit

switched to the flight-refuelling role, and Nos 138 and 7 Sqns disbanded at Wittering on 1 April and 30 September, respectively. Tony Cottingham's crew did the last No 7 Sqn QRA duty. 'There was a disbandment party that evening, and our QRA was scheduled to end at 2359 hrs. An hour or so before that we had a message that the Vulcan squadron taking over was not ready, and we were to continue on duty until something like 0800 hrs the next morning'. AOC No 3 Group referred to No 7 Sqn as 'the last of the Main Force Valiant squadrons'.

The Valiant tankers of Nos 214 and 90 Sqns did sterling service in the AAR role from 1962 to 1964. One particularly important mission was Operation *Chive* in March 1964, when tankers from both squadrons supported four Javelin Mk 9Rs, en route from Binbrook to Butterworth, across the Arabian Sea and Indian Ocean. Despite their offload limitations, the tankers were proving to be an indispensable asset to the RAF, with the new Belfast and VC10 strategic transport fleet being given probes to flight refuel from Valiants in emergencies.

Dave Morris joined No 90 Sqn at Honington as a first tour co-pilot in late 1963. He had no sooner arrived than he was helping take Javelins and Victors out to the Far East during the Malayan Confrontation. The standard eastabout route was via Malta, Masirah and Gan, although No 90 Sqn raised a few eyebrows when it escorted a Javelin formation through Karachi. 'We did things then we wouldn't dream of doing 15 years later', he recalled. 'There were no Go/No Go calculations – either you got airborne or you didn't. Even with the extra boost from water methanol injection, it could be touch and go. One hot day we just about got airborne from Idris, and when we checked later, our tyre tracks were in the sand at the upwind end of the runway'.

In May 1963 it was agreed that 'the SACEUR-assigned Valiants are planned to continue in service until the late 1960s'. The Valiant TBF, SR and tanker squadrons worked well until 6 August 1964, when

Upping the Alert State, the crew of a Valiant leap from the QRA Car and sprint to their aircraft. All they have to do now is to strap in, light up the engines and roll onto the runway

Flt Lt J W 'Taff' Foreman, a flying instructor at the Gaydon OCU, took off to instruct a student pilot in Valiant WP217. The climb out over Shropshire in cloud was uneventful. Dave Bradford was the Nav Radar, and as WP217 passed over Lake Vyrnwy approaching 30,000 ft, 'an enormous explosion shook the whole aircraft. There were no signs on the H2S of a mid-air collision, so we returned to Gaydon to burn off fuel down to below maximum normal landing weight of 110,000 lbs. Everything appeared to be normal, and as we came in to land 'Taff' Foreman lowered the flaps, but when the aircraft started to roll because the starboard flap wouldn't lower, he raised them again'.

WP217 landed flapless, but one wing sagged on landing and the crew was lucky to get down alive because the rear spar of the starboard mainplane had cracked in the air, shearing the starboard flap drive – if the flaps had lowered they would probably have torn the wing off. The trainee crew flew again in another Valiant the following day, but as hordes of Vickers and Farnborough men descended on Gaydon they soon found that WP217 was not the only airframe with problems. The whole fleet was grounded while a working party tried to discover the extent to which the Valiants were affected by metal fatigue. By the end of September all Valiants had been divided into three categories;

Cat A – Flyable to five per cent of remaining fatigue life (12 aircraft)

Cat B – Flyable in emergency (19 aircraft)

Cat C – Grounded (five aircraft)

As Dave Morris recalled, 'No 90 Sqn flew Cat A aircraft because it had AAR commitments. The captains flew together to stay current and a Chipmunk was brought in for the co-pilots!'

WZ374 of No 7 Sqn at Entebbe, when a two-ship detachment from the unit – which had officially disbanded on 30 September 1962 – flew out from Wittering to take part in Uganda's independence celebrations on 9 October. WZ374 was captained by Sqn Ldr Clayton and XD873 by Tony Cottingham. As Runway 36 was no longer in use at Entebbe, it acted as a Valiant dispersal. 'To get one aircraft past the other', recalled Tony Cottingham, 'we taxied up the edge of the runway and turned sharply to get the wing out of the way. When I did this on a hot afternoon, the tandem undercarriage screwed a hole down through the runway tarmac. We thus justified returning to the UK via Nairobi to avoid further surface damage with heavy aircraft at Entebbe' (*Tony Cottingham*)

Valiant B(PR)K 1 WZ376 refuels prototype Javelin FAW 9 XH965, the latter aircraft being flown from A&AEE Boscombe Down

Valiant B 1 XD870 was converted into a tanker in February 1958, before serving with No 214 Sqn until it was scrapped on 4 March 1965 (*Pete Sharp*)

A Sea Vixen FAW 1 of 899 Naval Air Squadron refuels Valiant XD858 on 16 April 1962, just to show that it could be done. The naval aircraft was being flown by Cdr D 'Shorty' Hamilton, who had initially carried out some 'plug-ins' on the Valiant at 30,000 ft. According to Hamilton, 'After I had finished I asked the pilot if he would like a go. The enterprising "crab" said yes. All I could see in my rearview mirror was the Valiant's windscreen!'

No 543 Sqn had had a foretaste of the impending troubles in July 1964 during Operation *Pontifex* over Southern Rhodesia when WZ394 'developed a crack in the rear spar which necessitated it being returned to base for repair'. After the squadron's eight B(PR) 1s had their rear spars inspected in October 1964, only two were found fit to remain in frontline service. WZ391 and XD826 were allowed to fly 12 hours per month for each of the five crews needed to meet the War Role in a national emergency.

By 2 October it was clear that the Valiant failures had occurred at between 35 per cent and 75 per cent of assessed safe fatigue life, which called into serious question the validity of existing Valiant fatigue data.

Bearing a red winged lion emblem on its fin tip, this No 207 Sqn Valiant was put on public display at Filton, in Bristol, shortly after it had been camouflaged

Being a relatively simple aeroplane, the Valiant relied for its strength on a massive 'backbone' member running along the top of the fuselage, with two branches at right angles on each side. These linked up with the two forged beams that acted as the front and rear wing spars, and it was these that had cracked. These huge spars carried the majority of the wing loads, and although they were large in size, an apparently small crack affecting a mere five per cent of the load-bearing area could result in a 30 per cent reduction in strength.

There are two generic types of aircraft structure – the Safe Life and the Fail Safe. The former is one that has low residual strength if a primary load-bearing member should fail, whereas the latter has alternative load paths so that if a primary load-bearing member cracks, residual strength remains because the loads can be assumed by adjacent members. In modern aircraft Fail Safe structures with up to three alternative load paths are provided, but back in 1947 the main load-bearing structure was Safe Life. This did not matter on an interim airframe designed for life in the calm upper air, but at 500 ft the loads and stresses were far more violent.

Manufacturers had done very little fatigue research because none was called for in the original specification, so the only advice given was that to transfer the V-bombers from a regime for which they had been designed to a totally different one would shorten their life. Low-level flying was generally treated as a service problem, and the RAF was left to sort it out. However, its engineers did not know how much safe life had already been used up by the Valiants, how much stress was imposed during any particular sortie, or how much stress a Valiant could take before it cracked under the strain.

Those airframes that were approaching the design life of 3000 hours were restricted in the number of low-level missions they could fly, but as one captain recalled, 'We did a lot on the Valiant through ignorance. Fatigue considerations never entered our heads as we did low-level high-speed runs over any old air traffic control tower before pulling up like a ding-bat'.

At first it was thought that the OCU aircraft would be the worst affected, for they were generally the oldest airframes. WP217, for example, had completed a full operational life on No 207 Sqn before being entrusted to OCU students. The low-level bomber squadrons were expected to be the next worst, followed by decreasing degrees of 'crackery' in the tankers, and ending with No 543 Sqn, which only flew gently about at high-level on reconnaissance duties. But as they examined the whole force, the engineers found that although the low-level squadrons certainly displayed the worst signs of strain, some tankers and reconnaissance aircraft were not much better off.

In their quest for better performance after 1945, aircraft engineers became very weight conscious, and they rejected the old wartime light aluminium alloys in preference to new high-strength, light zinc-bearing forged alloys known as DTD 683 and 687. These double heat-treated plates were extremely strong, as well as light, but in time the alloys tended to become brittle, with a high propensity for stress fatigue, corrosion and a high crack propagation rate. 'DTD 683 was a bad mistake by the Ministry of Supply', said one senior Vickers man, 'but we did not have the range of alternatives that we have today. If we had known then what

The crew chief holds the Form 700 as the captain of a camouflaged Valiant signs for his aircraft on the Marham ramp

we know now about DTD 683 we would not have used it, but if we hadn't used 683 the aircraft would have been much heavier, or we would have had a gap of seven to ten years before alternative materials became available to build an aeroplane that did as well as those Valiants'.

On 30 November approval was given for 40 Valiants to be repaired over a five-month period at a cost of around £250,000, but then in early December an inspection of one of the affected aircraft revealed a crack in the front spar bigger than that in the rear spar. Consequently, a signal was sent to Bomber Command on 9 December ordering the cessation of Valiant flying except in the event of a national emergency. However, the QRA commitment was maintained and crews allowed to start engines and taxi to test the systems in case of war.

A note on the Valiant force prepared for the Prime Minister in early January 1965 said that development of the airframe had cost £10 million, and that just over 100 Valiants had been bought for the RAF for £57 million. Since 1960 24 jets had been assigned to SACEUR with 48 American weapons, 16 converted to tankers and eight used in the SR role. The total number of Valiants, including those used for training and research, was currently 61. By 15 January, investigations had shown that 60 of these were suffering from fatigue damage, and the experts agreed that none of them 'could be cleared as fully safe to normal design standards for flight'. When the only two spare, unused, Valiant spars in existence were checked, they too were found to have stress cracks in them even though they had never flown!

The Air Force Board concluded that there was 'little alternative to withdrawing all the Valiants from service', and SACEUR was informed personally of the decision by C-in-C Bomber Command on 25 January. The following day No 543 Sqn was relieved of its war plan commitment as a signal went out from the MoD authorising the cessation of QRA, grounding the Valiants permanently and formally ending all Valiant training. John Foot was a navigator on the No 214 Sqn QRA crew. 'When the radio said it had been announced in Parliament that the Valiants were to be scrapped, a wife rang up and said, "What are you doing over there?" It was the first we had heard of it'.

'I well recall the end of the era', said Pete Sharp. 'It was a Saturday morning at about 1030 hrs, and I was on "Duty Crew". We were tasked with QRA support, and I recall picking up the phone in the Crew Room and being told to hand it over to the team leader, Chf Tech "Curly" Stoneman. He turned quite pale, then went quiet and put the phone down. He turned to us and said that he had just received an

The low-level scheme applied to the Valiant force in 1963-64 consisted of glossy polyurethane paint in dark green and medium sea grey, with the aircraft's serial number applied in black. The bombers retained their anti-flash white undersides

order to "Down Load" all QRA aircraft! The implications of this action were immediately obvious to us all. He picked up the phone again and rang Ops to verify the message, and then insisted on speaking to the Station Commander. The latter called back a short while later and verified the order. And so began the end. I worked on all three Vs in a long RAF career, but the Valiant was far more beautiful in my eyes than the vicious looking Victor or the shapely Vulcan'.

OC Gaydon, Gp Capt A H Chamberlain, noted in his ORB that the first Valiant OCU course had started there in February 1955, and 'since that time 1475 aircrew of all categories have been trained on Valiants, in addition to many hundreds passing through on refresher courses'. He noted that a decision was still awaited on disposal of Gaydon's four remaining Valiants.

On the other hand, OC Marham, Gp Capt P A Kennedy, pulled no punches in his ORB comments. 'The official news and the MoD announcement was numbing in both its effect at Marham and its matter-of-factness. Marham's contribution to NATO, which was by far the most powerful and reliable of any RAF station, was dismissed and great play was made of the loss of tankers. There is no doubt at Marham, or at Supreme HQ Allied Powers Europe, which is the greater loss. It is understood that one Valiant is to be preserved for historic purposes, but the future of the rest is not finally known'. Apart from a few aircraft kept flying for trials work, most Valiants suffered the ignominy of being blown up for scrap where they sat.

C-in-C Bomber Command, AM Sir John Grandy, sent the following personal signal to AOC No 3 Group on 27 January 1965. 'It is a bitter blow that the outcome of the Valiant troubles has had to be their withdrawal from service. As the first of the V-bombers, and the air- and groundcrews who have flown and maintained them, they have played a major role in the nation's defence for nearly ten years. I send to all ranks of the Valiant force past and present my congratulations on the excellent record that had been maintained with this fine aircraft throughout its service in the Royal Air Force'.

'This is causing considerable embarrassment for us with our NATO allies', said Defence Minister Denis Healey, for the Valiants gave SACEUR his only long-range heavy punch, and their removal left a large gap in his inventory. The RAF had to make hurried adjustments to absorb upwards of 300 aircrew, plus hundreds of specialised technicians, not to mention 'difficulties in respect of its in-flight refuelling and long-range photo-reconnaissance capabilities. Steps are in hand to accelerate the conversion of Victor aircraft for these roles. Meanwhile,

The bitter end. Valiants are broken up for scrap at Marham in January 1965, having seen less than a decade of operational service

adjustments have been made in the deployment of our fighters so as to permit overseas reinforcement, and Canberra photo-reconnaissance aircraft are being used to carry out as much as possible of the survey work that would have fallen to the Valiants'.

Thirteen different sub-sets of Valiant were produced in all, and they clocked up many firsts. Among the many other roles considered for the Valiant were anti-shipping strikes, using the Green Cheese anti-ship weapon then under development. This 4000-lb fully active homing bomb would have relied on the Valiant's NBS radar reconnaissance capability for search, location and identification. Minelaying from normal medium-bomber heights and speeds was also proposed.

Vickers re-sparred XD816 to check the feasibility of repairing the whole fleet, and the aircraft duly made the very last Valiant flight from Wisley to Abingdon in June 1968 for the RAF's 50th Anniversary celebration.

Looking back, the Valiant had no vices at all. Arthur Steele flew 42 types during his distinguished RAF career 'but the Valiant stands out as one of the most honest aircraft to handle – by that I mean you got the response you wanted, and it was a nice, pleasant aircraft to fly – not all aircraft are like that'. 'It was one of the few aircraft', declared another pilot nostalgically, 'which all who have flown it speak of only with affection', and this was all the more remarkable given that it paved the way without the benefit of the experience of others. Sir George Edwards recalled that Vickers was 'given no mercy because we could not build flying scale models – it had to be right first time', and the fact that it was right, and appeared at the right time for the right price, demonstrated everything that was great about the British aviation industry.

It is said that every post-war Boeing airliner is based on the Valiant's USAF counterpart, the B-47 bomber. That is as maybe, but if you live under the approach to Heathrow airport you are just as likely to see planforms that cry out 'Vickers Valiant'. This simple design of genius was so versatile that it could undoubtedly have been developed further. Although the Valiant B 1 was limited by the size of its geometrically restricted bays to engines of up to 11,000 lbs thrust, Weybridge proposed a re-design with Conways that would have cost no more than the improvements Avro and Handley Page were funded to carry out with the Mk 2 Vulcan and Victor.

As for the Pathfinder Valiant B 2, this was structurally capable of low-level speeds far in excess of those sustained by low-level strike Vulcans and Victors. Although they were separated by 20 years, the Valiant B 2 had a low-level cruising speed similar to that of the Rockwell B-1, which the US developed at an original cost of $2700 million to keep in the manned bombing business.

With hindsight, Bomber Command and the nation might been better off if the RAF had bought only the high-level Valiant B 1 as an interim aircraft, followed by the Valiant B 2 as the advanced airframe with refined electronics – they need not have bothered with the Vulcan or Victor at all. It is a fascinating thought, and perhaps if Vickers had not been so good at building other aircraft, or had sited their factories in more economically depressed regions of the UK, a Valiant might still be flying today.

APPENDICES

VALIANT SQUADRONS

No 232 OCU – Formed Gaydon 21 February 1955 to train Valiant B 1 aircrew. B Flight converted to the Valiant while A Flight converted to the Victor B 1 after November 1957 and, eventually, C Flight to the Victor B 2. The Valiant Flight of No 232 OCU disbanded in February 1965.

No 7 Sqn – Re-formed Honington 1 November 1956 with Valiant B(PR) 1 to September 1962, B 1 and B(K) 1 January 1957 to September 1962. Moved to Wittering 26 July 1960, B(PR)K 1 August 1961 to May 1962. Disbanded 30 September 1962, though one Flight was kept in being to take part in the Ugandan independence celebrations (constellation Ursa Major insignia).

No 18 Sqn – Re-formed Finningley 17 December 1958 from C Flight No 199 Sqn with Valiant B 1. Disbanded 31 March 1963 (Pegasus rampant insignia).

No 49 Sqn – Re-formed Wittering 1 May 1956 with Valiant B 1 to March 1963, B(PR) 1 June 1956 to November 1956, B(K) 1 November 1956 to December 1964. Moved to Marham 26 June 1961, disbanded 1 May 1965 (greyhound running insignia).

No 90 Sqn – Re-formed Honington 1 January 1957, with Valiant B(K) 1 from March 1957 to December 1964, B(PR) 1 March 1957 to December 1960, B(PR)K 1 from May 1957 to March 1961. Disbanded 1 March 1965 (hind insignia).

No 138 Sqn – Re-formed Gaydon 1 January 1955 with Valiant B 1 to March 1962. Moved to Wittering 6 July 1955, B(PR) 1 March 1956 to May 1961, B(PR)K 1 March 1956 to August 1961, B(K) 1 June 1956 to April 1962. Disbanded 1 April 1962 (a sword in bend, the point uppermost severing a reef knot insignia).

No 148 Sqn – Re-formed Marham 1 July 1956 with Valiant B(K) 1 to December 1964, B 1 December 1956 to December 1964, B(PR) 1 December 1957 to December 1964, B(PR)K 1 February 1958 to December 1964. Disbanded 1 May 1965 (two battle axes in saltire insignia).

No 199 Sqn – Valiant B 1 at Honington from 29 May 1957. Renumbered No 18 Sqn at Finningley 17 December 1958 (two swords, one pointing upwards and the other downwards, in front of a fountain insignia).

No 207 Sqn – Re-formed Marham 1 April 1956 with Valiant B(PR) 1 and B(K) 1 to December 1964, B 1 March 1962 to December 1964. Disbanded 1 May 1965 (winged lion insignia).

No 214 Sqn – Re-formed Marham 21 January 1956 with Valiant B(PR) 1 to December 1957, B 1 March 1956 to November 1957, B(PR)K 1 April 1956 to December 1964 and B(K) 1 January 1957 to December 1964. Disbanded 1 March 1965 (nightjar in flight insignia).

No 543 Sqn – Re-formed Gaydon 1 April 1955 with Valiant B(PR) 1 to December 1964. Moved to Wyton 18 November 1955, B(PR)K 1 February 1956 to December 1964 (crane with open padlock in its beak insignia).

COLOUR PLATES

1

Valiant Type 667 WB215, de Havilland Hatfield, 1956

The second prototype, which came off the line on 11 April 1952, WB215 was modified for the London-New Zealand Air Race in 1953. On 17 November 1955 it was allocated to undertake Super Sprite RATOG trials, as depicted in this profile. WB215 suffered an accident at A&AEE Boscombe Down on 29 April 1957 and at the end of that year it was broken up during wing fatigue tests after flying just 489 hours.

2

Valiant B 1 WP206 of No 138 Sqn, RAF Gaydon, 1955

The first production Valiant B 1 delivered to the RAF on 8 February 1955, WP206 was put into service in the standard RAF lightweight matt aluminium 'high-speed silver' finish. It moved to No 49 Sqn on 5 June 1956 and then went to Marshalls of Cambridge for Blue Steel missile development work. The bomber left the UK on 12 October 1961 for Blue Steel trials at Edinburgh Field, South Australia, returning to the UK on 27 May 1963. It was sold for scrap on 16 February 1964.

3

Valiant BK 1 XD875 of No 138 Sqn, RAF Wittering, 1961

XD875 was the last Valiant to be delivered to the RAF, the aircraft joining No 49 Sqn on 24 September 1957. It took part in the SAC Bombing Competition in 1958 before returning to the UK to join No 207 Sqn on 23 October 1958. The bomber moved to No 138 Sqn on 26 June 1961, and it is depicted here with the unit's crest (a sword severing a reef knot) on the tail. XD875 moved to No 7 Sqn on 16 April 1962, and it was written off on 9 November that same year after an accident. The nose of the bomber is preserved in Inverness.

4

Valiant B(PR) 1 WZ399 of No 543 Sqn, RAF Wyton, 1957

WZ399 joined No 543 Sqn on 5 October 1956, and it is seen here in a high-visibility 'Snow Trip' colour scheme. The crew abandoned takeoff at Offutt AFB on 3 November 1961, whereupon WZ399 overran the runway and crossed a main highway, before coming to rest on a railway embankment. The aircraft subsequently burnt out, but the crew survived because the cockpit broke off and catapulted across the railway line.

5

Valiant B(PR) 1 WZ392 of No 543 Sqn, RAF Wyton, 1959

Depicted here sporting No 543 Sqn's crane motif on its port underwing drop tank, WZ392 was delivered new to Wyton on 4 April 1956. It remained here until struck off charge on 3 March 1965 after amassing 2265 flying hours.

6

Valiant B(PR)K 1 WZ380 of No 543 Sqn, RAF Wyton, 1963

WZ380 was delivered to the RAF on 13 February 1956, and it undertook 'Snow Trip' trials in Canada. Shown here in low visibility markings with pale serials and the crane badge on the fin, the aircraft remained assigned to No 543 Sqn until struck off charge on 3 March 1965, with 2470 flying hours on the clock.

7

Valiant BK 1 XD814 of No 148 Sqn, RAF Marham, 1956

XD814, depicted here in high-speed silver finish with a black and grey radome and night anti-glare panels, was the first Valiant to bomb at Suez. It subsequently served with Nos 138 and 90 Sqns, before receiving low-level camouflage in February 1964. XD814 was struck off charge on 15 December that same year.

8

Valiant BK 1 XD818 of No 49 Sqn, RAF Wittering, 1957

XD818 was delivered to Wittering on 14 December 1956. It subsequently dropped the first *Grapple* bomb whilst being flown by the Hubbard crew. The aircraft is depicted here in the all-white anti-flash Titanine paint scheme. XD818 came back to No 49 Sqn from the Pacific and then went with the squadron to Marham. Struck off charge on 1 March 1965, the bomber now resides in the Cold War Museum at RAF Cosford following several decades in the Bomber Command Museum at RAF Hendon.

9

Valiant BK 1 XD826 of No 7 Sqn, RAF Honington, 1958

After undertaking probe trials with Flight Refuelling Ltd, XD826 was delivered to No 7 Sqn on 12 February 1957. Shown here in the high-speed silver finish, with No 7 Sqn's Ursa Major crest on the fin, XD826 moved across to No 90 Sqn on 19 July 1960 and then to No 138 Sqn at Wittering on 16 October 1961. It joined No 232 OCU at Gaydon on 24 April 1962 and was struck off charge on 4 March 1965.

10

Valiant B(PR) 1 WZ377 of No 90 Sqn, RAF Honington, 1958

WZ377 was delivered to No 543 Sqn on 29 December 1955. It later moved to No 232 OCU and then back to No 543 Sqn, before serving with Nos 214, 90 and 7 Sqns. The bomber eventually returned to No 232 OCU on 18 August 1961, and it was struck off charge on 1 March 1965.

11

Valiant B 1 WP213 of No 199 Sqn, RAF Honington, 1957

Delivered to No 138 Sqn on 2 April 1955, WP213 went to Watton for installation of ECM equipment on 29 August 1956, then on to No 199 Sqn on 29 May 1957 and No 18 Sqn on 16 December 1958. It moved to No 19 Maintenance Unit at St Athan on 14 April 1963 and was scrapped on 6 April 1965.

12

Valiant BK 1 XD816 of No 214 Sqn, RAF Marham, 1960

XD816 joined No 148 Sqn on 3 September 1956, moved to No 214 Sqn on 4 March 1958 and was then sent for conversion into a K 1 tanker at Marshalls eight months later. After other test work, it went back to No 214 Sqn on 10 June 1959. Note the aircraft's tail insignia comprising No 214 Sqn's badge and the trademark of Flight Refuelling Ltd. This emblem was first introduced by the unit in 1961. XD816 was used for the trial installation of a rear spar repair scheme at Wisley in October 1964, being re-sparred in November 1965. The aircraft was finally struck off charge on 26 August 1970 after 2012 flight hours and 829 landings. Parts of it are now on display at the RAF Hendon Museum .

13

Valiant B(PR) 1 WP217 of No 232 OCU, RAF Gaydon, 1964

Delivered to A Flight of No 543 Sqn on 11 May 1955, WP217 subsequently joined No 207 Sqn at Marham on 8 August 1957, No 7 Sqn on 15 February 1960 and No 232 OCU at Gaydon on 21 November 1960. Shown here in low conspicuity white finish, the bomber suffered a catastrophic starboard mainplane failure while in a climb on 6 August 1964. WP217 never flew again, being struck off charge 11 days later.

14

Valiant B! WZ365 of No 18 Sqn, RAF Finningley, 1959

Carrying No 18 Sqn's winged Pegasus marking on its fin, WZ365 was originally delivered new to No 232 OCU on 22 September 1955 – the aircraft took part in that year's Farnborough airshow. It joined No 199 Sqn on 17 June 1957 and went for RCM conversion at Watton, where it remained until 1 November 1957. WZ365 was repaired at Wisley after a minor accident, before returning to No 18 Sqn on 22 June 1959. Sent to St Athan for storage on 19 April 1963, the bomber was scrapped on 16 June 1965.

15

Valiant BK 1 WZ400 of the BCDU, RAF Wittering, 1961

WZ400 joined No 138 Sqn on 2 June 1956 and subsequently moved to the BCDU on 9 June 1959.

The bomber rejoined No 138 Sqn on 30 September 1959, before completing its RAF service with the BCDU from 25 February 1960. In store at St Athan on 4 December 1962, WZ400 was sold for scrap on 1 January 1967.

16

Valiant B(PR) 1 WZ378 of No 7 Sqn, RAF Wittering, 1961

WZ378 joined No 214 Sqn on 4 January 1956, moved to No 49 Sqn on 2 July that same year and finally joined No 7 Sqn on 16 May 1957. Sent to St Athan for storage on 12 October 1962, it was scrapped on 16 June 1965.

17

Valiant BK 1 XD872 of No 90 Sqn, RAF Honington, 1962

Delivered to the RAF on 28 June 1957 for tropical trials, XD872 had a Sprite RATOG engine torn off in flight exactly one week later. Also used in maximum takeoff weight flight trials, the bomber finally commenced frontline service when it joined No 138 Sqn on 13 January 1958. The aircraft moved to the BCDU for tropical trials over Libya and then joined No 7 Sqn on 25 August 1961. XD872 was transferred to No 90 Sqn on 19 December 1961, and remained with the unit until it was sent to BAC Filton on 19 October 1964 and subsequently struck off charge on 10 June 1965.

18

Valiant B(PR) 1 WP219 of No 207 Sqn, RAF Marham, 1961

WP219 joined No 543 Sqn on 16 June 1955 and was transferred to No 207 Sqn on 26 June 1956. It stayed with the latter unit throughout its service career, apart from detachments to Farnborough and Boscombe Down in 1962 and 1963, respectively, for bombing trials. The aircraft was scrapped on 1 March 1965.

19

Valiant B 2 WJ954, Vickers Weybridge, 1953

The all-black Type 673 Pathfinder came into being in time for the 1953 Farnborough airshow. After flying for just 167 hours, it was struck off charge on 18 March 1958 and dismantled at Wisley.

20

Valiant BK 1 WZ404 of No 207 Sqn, RAF Marham, 1964

Delivered to No 207 Sqn on 30 June 1956, WZ404 remained with the unit throughout its career. The bomber is show here in the low-level, glossy polyurethane camouflage of dark green and medium sea grey (with serial numbers in black) that was applied in 1963-64. WZ404 was scrapped at Marham on 1 March 1965 after amassing 2614 flying hours.

21

Valiant BK 1 XD825 of No 49 Sqn, RAF Marham, 1964

XD825 joined No 49 Sqn on 30 November 1956

and took part in *Grapple* tests in 1958. Apart from a short spell with No 543 Sqn from 21 January to 7 May 1959, it remained with No 49 Sqn throughout its service life of 2351 flying hours. Illustrated here in low-level camouflage finish, XD825 took part in an inner mainplane repair scheme after 1 April 1965, before being struck off charge on 10 June that same year.

BIBLIOGRAPHY

Aldrich, Richard, *GCHQ*, HarperPress, 2010

Brookes, Andrew, *Photo Reconnaissance*, Ian Allan, 1975

Brookes, Andrew, *The V-force*, The History of Britain's Airborne Deterrent, Jane's, 1982

Hennessy, Peter, *Having It So Good – Britain in the Fifties*, Allen Lane, 2006

Hubbard, Kenneth and Simmons, Michael, *Operation Grapple,* Ian Allan, 1985

Jefford C G, *RAF Squadrons*, Airlife, 2001

Lee, Sir David, *Wings in the Sun*, HMSO, 1989

Morgan, Eric B, *Vickers Valiant*, Aerofax, 2002

RAF Historical Society Journals No 28, 2003 and No 39, 2007

Walker, John R, *British Nuclear Weapon Stockpiles 1953-78*, RUSI Journal Vol 156 No 5, October/November 2011

Wynn, Humphrey, *RAF Nuclear Deterrent Forces*, HMSO, 1994

INDEX